THE WHITE MAN'S BURDEN

A DISCUSSION OF THE INTERRACIAL QUESTION
WITH SPECIAL REFERENCE TO THE RE-
SPONSIBILITY OF THE WHITE RACE
TO THE NEGRO PROBLEM

BY

B. F. RILEY, D. D., LL.D.

"They are slaves who fear to speak,
For the friendless and the weak;
They are slaves who fear to be
In the right with two or three."
—LOWELL.

ISBN: 978-1-63923-783-8

Printed: March 2023

Published and Distributed By:
Lushena Books
607 Country Club Drive, Unit E
Bensenville, IL 60106
www.lushenabks.com

ISBN: 978-1-63923-783-8

TO ALL
LOVERS OF RIGHT AND LIBERTY,
ALL
FRIENDS OF HUMANITY,
IRRESPECTIVE OF CLASS OR CONDITION.

"REMEMBER that to change thy opinion, and to follow him who corrects thy error, is as consistent with freedom as it is to persist in thy error."

MARCUS AURELIUS.

"THERE is no ignorance more shameful than to admit as true that which one does not understand; and there is no advantage so great as that of being set free from error."

SOCRATES.

"SIT DOWN before a fact as a little child, be prepared to give up every preconceived notion, follow humbly wherever and to whatever abysses nature leads, or you will learn nothing."

HUXLEY.

"I STAND to God and my country."

MOTTO OF THE SCOTCH LORD ASTON.

TABLE OF CONTENTS

INTRODUCTION.

A general review of the work—Its purpose—Advantages enjoyed by the Author in its preparation—Repression a failure in all governments—Prompt action demanded—Certain difficulties increasing—The part which the Negro will take—The interest of civilization one for all social groups—England's example—Conciliation her policy for more than a century—Hon. James Bryce quoted...9

CHAPTER I.

The Question Stated.

The great race problem—A critical juncture reached—The contribution of the saloon to the race question—Corrupt politics —How shifting changes have aggravated the inter-racial question—Certain sociological elements—Futile proposals—The Negro's progress—Compared with the Hebrews—Negro progress phenomenal—Surpasses that of all other enslaved races—A trumpet call for aid..17

CHAPTER II.

Genesis of the Negro Problem.

What it is—It began 258 years ago—The Negro not responsible —A brief survey of Negro servitude—How the problem has grown from the beginning of slavery—The discovery of America —How it facilitated African slavery—Both North and South shared in it—The Negro a passive instrument—How the problem ripened for two and a half centuries—The Negro not a voluntary foreign immigrant—In America by coercion—Who is responsible? 28

CHAPTER III.

The Higher Law.

Agency of Providence—Slavery an object of gain—The hand of Providence shown—God not mocked—Cruelty of slavery and its fruit—The ripening harvest—Providence reigns above human law—"Chickens come home to roost"—Treatment accorded the Negro after using him over 250 years—A responsibility on both North and South—Injustice done the Negro because he is one— Justice must ultimately reign—God demands an observance of His laws—Sooner or later Providence will be heard 39

CHAPTER IV.

The Southern Negro as He Is.

A calm presentation of the matter—Superior and inferior Negroes—How that was demonstrated on Southern plantations during the regime of slavery—How it found expression after emancipation—Negro leaders—Men of force and character—Accomplishments in the face of odds—Harbingers of racial progress—A perpetual inspiration to the race—Their desert of encouragement—The middle class, or yeomanry—Their rugged character—Their hope in their children—How imposed on—Their drawbacks—Peculiar struggles—Mistaken motives of life—Need of moral direction—The criminal class—How it involves the entire race in the public mind—All held responsible for the deeds of the few—Our duty even to the base class—We must lift, or they will lower..................................50

CHAPTER V.

Are We Debtors to the Negro?

A candid consideration needed—Prejudice a serious barrier to judgment—Misunderstandings—What the Negro has done for the white race—His industry enriches the country—Seven generations of whites educated by the Negro slave—The country transformed by his toil and sweat—Turned loose without a penny—His loyalty and devotion in time of war—How has he been compensated?—An appeal to gratitude and justice—The Negro's efforts to rise to better things—Injustice in the courts—Injustice on common carriers—Dangers thicken—We cannot close our eyes to the facts..................................61

CHAPTER VI.

The Negro's Share in Building the Nation.

His loyalty and patriotism during the Revolution—Crispus Attucks, a Negro, the first to fall in the cause—Peter Salem kills the British commander—Prince, a Negro, captures General Prescott—Negro troops in the Revolution—General Jackson's appeal to the Negroes of Louisiana—The Negro during the Civil War—Chief characteristic of the Negro—Alexander Stephens' "corner-stone speech"—What the country was and is, and the Negro's share in its development—Our duty in the premises 74

CHAPTER VII.

Serious Barriers to Negro Progress.

His previous servitude against him—Unrequited labors forgotten in a period of prejudice—Advantage taken of his condition—The Negro in history—His success disputed at every step—His claims unheeded—His onward march of progress—Bad deeds exploited and good deeds unnoticed—What he has been able to accomplish..................................88

CHAPTER VIII.

Value of the Negro to Our Civilization.

What is the Negro worth to the country?—A financial estimate—How has he proved his value?—Compared with other laborers—He is the laborer for the South—No other can take his place—A means of protection to our civilization—Strong reasons for giving him a fair chance in life—This is all he asks—What he has already done—What he can do if encouraged—A helper and not a hinderer—He deserves consideration—Shall he have it?
..................................100

CHAPTER IX.

A Force of Conservation.

His supposed weaknesses his real strength—His lack of undue assertion has saved him—Resistance would have destroyed him —Compared with the Indian—What the Negro has endured— His loyalty to the white race—His adjustability to conditions— While timid and docile, he has succeeded—His subdued temperament—Never occasions strikes—Never disloyal to the flag —Has compelled recognition of his worth.....................119

CHAPTER X.

Negro Womanhood.

What woman is to a race or nation—Negro woman no exception—Advantage taken of slave women—Vicious prostitution—Their estimate of the whites as models—The sad results on the race—Hope of the Negro race reposes in its womanhood —Industry and womanhood — Virtue applauded—Virtuous womanhood on the increase—The idea of home—No real home during Negro servitude—The idea had to be created after freedom—Genuine missionary effort needed......................131

CHAPTER XI.

A Call for Christian Humanitarianism.

Are we conscious of our obligation to a race of millions?— The Negro is here to stay—Shall we make the best or worst of him?—What the South is doing educationally—Prejudice to Negro education—Errors exploded—Illustrations of unreasonable injustice and cruelty—Ethiopia stretches forth her hands—Race aversion antagonistic to the Christian spirit 142

CHAPTER XII.

Mob Violence.

What it is—How it began with the Negro—Passes original boundaries—Lawlessness begets lawlessness—Crime avenged by crime—Whites are falling victims as a logical consequence— Grounds claimed for lynching—Arguments for lynching exploded —The mob a menace to society—Illustrations offered in proof— Tendency toward chaotic conditions—The Atlanta Constitution and Courier-Journal quoted.................................153

CHAPTER XIII.

What Can Be Done?

A plan proposed—A national movement needed—An organization with appropriate departments—A tremendous and difficult task—Our civilization involved—Illustrations drawn from foreign missions—A concrete situation—Intensely practical condition—What can be done for the Negro for the good of both races?—A juncture of eras—Demand for genuine manhood— Senator Revels quoted—A movement fraught with promise— Will we recognize our present duty and opportunity? 165

CHAPTER XIV.

Sources of Encouragement.

The present condition invites to benevolent activity—The situation encouraging—The Negro ready and responsive—A reformation possible—What the Negro has done unaided—What he can do if helped—Negligence and prejudice—Destined results —How much the Negro has achieved—Unknown and unrecognized—Bishop Galloway quoted—A mistaken course—Strike against the Negro on the Georgia Railroad—Its lessons—A wholesome judgment rendered — The press quoted — Judge Lovett, successor to Mr. Harriman, on the Southern Negro...181

CHAPTER XV.

Groundless Theories of Apprehension.

Predictions of the past compared with the facts of the present —False alarms displaced by wholesome facts—Imaginary troubles unrealized—Facts disprove ill-founded predictions— Worth established by many thousands of Negroes—Possessions of the Negro identify him with common interests—Depression of one race depresses the other—Negro rivalry a bugbear— Social equality idea ill-founded—The value of the thrifty and educated Negro—The source of certain apprehensions—Worthy Negroes never occasion trouble—The demand to make more of them worthy 197

CHAPTER XVI.

Omens of Promise.

Inspiration derived from the past—A wise leadership—Can the Negro be relied on?—"Still achieving, still pursuing"—Sentiment toward the Negro race gradually changing for the better— To what it is due—Reaction slowly setting in—The real friend of the Negro—The National Negro Business League—What it has done for the race—The Clifton Conference—Mr. W. N. Hartshorn—Efforts of the worthy Negro to raise the fallen of the race—Ignorance of what each race is doing a serious asset —A calm review of the situation needed—What will American Christianity do? 208

CHAPTER XVII.

A New Demand for an "Age of Reason."

Dispassionate consideration needed—Certain portentous signs —Possible dangers—Various theories—Embody their own means of failure—Responsibility supreme—Time for cool action—The Negro progressing, not receding—Friendliness of spirit—Respect for the future—Spirit of the Anglo-Saxon—Two prospective civilizations—Now or never.................................215

INTRODUCTION

The situation in the South has been presented in the following chapters, as the writer has seen it for a period of years. He claims that the advantage of being on the ground, as a close student of the existing situation, gives him at least some advantage in the presentation of his views, and a claim to be heard regarding a problem which has so long afflicted our people. From its numerous sides the problem has been often presented, but oftener than otherwise, from view-points of prejudice or partisanship. It betokens signs more favorable, however, that in the most recent works which have appeared on the subjcet, from the pens of representatives of both races, sentiments have assumed a milder and more assuring tone, while they have not been without the abatement of firmness and candor. It is also gratifying that the extravagance which has characterized so much of the literature adverse to the Negro in the past, is losing its popularity among the people of the South, thousands of whom happen to know that many of the statements which have been made are, to say the least, exaggerated.

The assumption of encouraging proportions by a question so grave, seems to call for a more comprehensive treatment of the vital features of the problem. In the present discussion the writer has laid stress on those features, instead of giving a summary view of the entire subject, as has been so frequently done. The present task has been actuated from a genuine desire to perform a humanitarian and patriotic duty. A son of an original slave holder, and a native of the South, the writer has been impelled to the performance of a task which has involved a painstaking investigation of the facts before they were committed to record. He knows whereof he speaks.

The conclusions at which he has arrived may not be concurred in by many, but they seem logical and just to a diligent student of affairs, and to possess some merit above those which are founded largely on theory. Exceptions may be taken to some of the views expressed, alike by representatives of both races. This is to be expected in view of the consideration of so many phases of a grave and momentous problem.

Throughout the discussion the writer has been impelled by an honest desire to present the truth in unvarnished form, with studious abstinence alike from exaggeration or extenuation. Impelled by a spirit of absolute candor, and divested of even the semblance of passion at any point, the facts have been sought to be presented as they are known. Around two chief facts are all the rest gathered, one of which is that the burden of this mighty problem lies at the door of the white race, and the other is that practical action in the attempted solution of the difficulty should no longer be delayed. The task is undoubtedly a tremendous one, and the period of its performance must be one of long transition, but it would seem that on account of these facts, a direct effort at solution should not longer be delayed. Continued inaction only invites the possibility of fresher complications, and if the matter is to receive the comprehensiveness of attention which it would seem to merit, and even to invite, nothing is to be gained by delay.

It must be clear to those interested in the situation that a policy of racial repression can never alleviate conditions, but the rather will serve to aggravate them. It is equally clear that difficulties in the way of even partial solution cannot be removed by bringing to the undertaking existing prejudice or preconceived notions unfavorable to the Negro. Genuine magnanimity from a stronger to a weaker race must be the first stepping-stone in the ascent to a final solution. Notions may have to be revamped and opinions changed, but this should not be difficult in the face of facts, duty, and absolute necessity, all of which at present seem urgent.

With every instinct of his being, the writer shares in the abhorrence of the atrocious crimes so often claimed to be committed, but he sees no relief by answering crime with crime. Every one should know that that means only continued aggravation and demoralization. Until we come to see eye to eye on a tremendous problem—until we approach it with calmness and dispassion, nothing can be done. Concession is not demanded by the present situation, only unbiased consideration. This is not asking too much, seeing what is involved in the industrial, educational, political, social and moral aspects of the question. While the Negro must not be remiss or inactive, and while he must work out his own destiny, he cannot do so successfully without the aid and co-operation of the best elements of the white race. Because of the complicated relations now existing, the aid of the whites is indispensable.

The concrete fact which confronts us is that the Negro is here ten million strong and is constantly growing stronger or more numerous. No matter who may now wish it were otherwise, the fact remains. We must not toy with theory, but face a fact—a vital and mighty condition. If the question be raised, What can be done? let patriotism, philanthropy, chivalry and Christianity answer. There is no hurt which can come to the Negro without seriously involving our civilization. The Negro is now so interlaced into American life that he must be considered an important part thereof. To heed the suggestion to let things drift and permit the matter to work itself out, is only the putting off of the evil day. The better part of soberness and wisdom is squarely to face the situation, realize its length and breadth, and respond to its demands. The subject

THE WHITE MAN'S BURDEN

cannot be dismissed as unworthy by a taunt or sneer, for it must remain in vital and inseparable contact with American life. Nor must we lose sight of the obligation which is imposed on the white race, which is solely responsible for the presence of the black man in America.

To contribute to the interest of the Negro, is to contribute, at the same time, to the interest of the public weal of which he is a part. To accomplish the most for him as well as for ourselves, the policy must be one of construction and not of destruction, for a policy of destruction is a two-edged sword which cuts both ways. Action toward another or others is reaction toward ourselves. We cannot escape the fact that the destinies of both races are inseparably bound together, and the task now imposed is to find a way which will be equally productive of good to both races. Nothing less than the development of each race will produce this result, for "manhood in a democracy is the essential basis of participation."

To claim that we cannot see what can be done, should excite to diligence for a proper course to be pursued, but to say that nothing can be done, is to acknowledge for the first time, in the history of the Anglo-Saxon, his inability to grapple with a great problem. The wrecks of difficulties overcome and shattered lie along the centuries of his history. In his aggressive march over the world the Anglo-Saxon has met a condition in America unencountered in the past stages of his history—that of fusing into a symmetrical government dissimilar elements under conditions which will bring them into harmonious adjustment to a flexible governmental policy, and of according to each his due proportion of liberty and justice. The demand of the highest constructive statesmanship will be needed to effect this, but where so much has been done by the white man, and in ways so many, the task, however difficult, can be accomplished. We have tried the effect of drastic legislation, and know what it is. This has always failed as a governmental policy, even where it is autocratic. Force may repress, but it is like the suppression of a volcano.

Long ago England pursued a policy of repression and coercion, but signally failing, she wisely turned to a basis of conciliation, as one of her greatest statesmen persuaded her to do in dealing with the American colonies. She is even now encountering difficulty in a conciliatory policy which is attempted in the federation of the South African states, where the sullen Dutch spirit so much at variance with British rule, stubbornly resists; but England recognizes that a policy must be discovered by means of which the recalcitrant elements must be brought into friendly and easy relations with the powers that be, and she will not fail to discover such a policy. The United States has a somewhat similar condition in its Philippine possessions, where aid of a substantial character must be rendered for years, and the courtship of a friendly spirit must go on, in order to win the natives to the dominant American sentiment. Compared with either of these, the conditions differ materially with respect to the ten million Negroes, but the one cardinal principle alike underlies all. It is as the Honorable James Bryce has suggested, "Duty and policy are one,'for it is equally to the interest of both races (in America) that their relations should be friendly."

One decided advantage seems to lie on the side of America in dealing with the present perplexing question. Both races, white and black, have suffered, and seriously suffered, in the transition crucible of long years. Like all suffering, this has not been unattended by lessons of value alike to both races. Each understood the other in the relation of master to slave; but when this relation was shifted to a novel orbit, complications arose. Here we encountered a grave problem, and it remains to this day. It is not necessary that we here descend into the details of that problem, to set forth which in its essential features, this little volume has been written. To meet the issue squarely as men and Christian patriots, is our present duty.

THE WHITE MAN'S BURDEN

CHAPTER I

THE QUESTION STATED

For almost a half century the colossal race question of the South has absorbed much public thought, given rise to endless discussion, and produced not a little speculation as to its final settlement. The comprehensiveness and manysidedness of the question have afforded the amplest opportunity alike for serious thought, fervid debate, and the wildest speculation. The "new racial cosmopolitanism" induced by the sudden transitions which followed the close of the Civil War, the methods of its creation, and the means of its management have occasioned sufficient friction and complication to produce a most serious problem.

Emancipation with its attendant consequences—the delight with which it was hailed as a boon by the millions of the enslaved, equalled only by the dismay with which a mighty industrial system was witnessed by the original slave owner to collapse; the unpreparedness of many thousands of the late slaves to prize the meaning of freedom, and the demand for labor on the farms of the South at a critical juncture;

the hilarity, on the one hand, of the former slave, and the sting of defeat, and sense of appalling loss on the part of the planter on the other, within themselves produced initial complications of no mean dimensions. But when added to these were other complications which dwarfed the former, the tension of difficulty at the South was at the highest taut. No matter what entered into the original conception of the reconstruction of affairs at the South, and there were no doubt both of vindictive animus and of sincerity of purpose to accomplish good—both of the plan to punish and humiliate the South, and to protect the Negro in his new-born rights, the result proved, for a time at least, disastrous to the settlement of the race question. The occasion was productive of a brood of political miscreants, alike from both sections, who took advantage of the untrained masses of Negroes by arraying them in hostility against their former owners.

There is another element which is invariably lost sight of in the treatment of this critical period, and yet without which it is doubtful if the breach between the two races in the South would have been so serious. The drinking den from which the Negro as a slave was restrained alike by legal statute and by the severe discipline of the plantation, was one of the most efficacious factors in the profound disturbance of the reconstruction period. It was found that the Negro was not easily pitted against his former master, and this arrayal was an indispensable adjunct of the fell purpose of this unconscionable horde of politicians, derived alike from the North and the South, until the saloon was laid under tribute. In recognition of this palpable fact the Negro leaders throughout the South today are among the most hostile elements of the saloon, and never lose an opportunity to deal it a deadly blow. Inflamed by cheap liquor, which was sold at every cross-road in the South, the Negro was more easily manipulated against the white race, and strife and bitterness were more readily engendered than they would have otherwise been. This bitterness and strife have been prolonged into the years of the future, and have been the occasion of creating other difficulties as they have gone on their way through a period of almost a half century.

These statements are bare historical facts which lie on the surface of that dark period of Southern history. At a time when irritation in the Southern mind was fresh, this most unfortunate condition was introduced, and had much to do with the dark troubles which followed. Not that all the recent slaves were thus easily betrayed into the hands of the saloon, for even at this time there were men among them who deplored the condition induced, and who threw themselves into the breach in loud protestation of this inroad of vice on the race. The natural anxiety of the Negro to assert his right by the use of the ballot, which assertion was stimulated by the means already named, was met by a hostile demonstration on the part of the whites, who were quickened by racial antipathy and a desire to pre-serve their institutions from the sway of the un-scrupulous political plunderer. The reign of terror which ensued is known and appreciated by those who were in the thick of the troubles of that period. Another element much to the disadvantage of the Negro entered into the period : While emancipation was generally recognized as a fixed fact, there were those who believed that the proper relation of the Negro was one of servitude, and that out of that element he was outside his natural sphere. The result was much harshness of treatment and conse-quent disorder. Even at that early period there was the absence of discrimination, as between the good and bad Negro, as there is today. The good among them, of whom there were not a few, were forced by an indiscriminate public sentiment to share in all the blameworthiness of the worst. The continuance of that sentiment has acted as a most serious barrier to the aspiring Negro since the era of emancipation. The reference to faults and crimes is often made in such way against the Negro as a race, rather than against the single offender, as to occasion much dis-satisfaction. The manifest unfairness of such whole-sale allusion seems never to have occurred to those who, in exploiting the failures and shortcomings of some, include the many, who by every commend-able means are seeking to rise in the scale of being.

With the gradual passing of the last generation of

slaves and slave holders came a new crisis. As has been shown, a broad breach had been created at the most inauspicious period of the Negro's history. Fresh from the fields of bondage, without equipment of mental strength or moral force, poor, with natural ambition benumbed and practically obliterated by long servitude, the Negro in an emergency like this, needed a friendly hand to guide and a kind voice to cheer. His was at this time a race of dependence, a people in their childhood. Could it have been possible for the passion of the time to have been displaced by friendship, could the pretended aid rendered by the worst of politicians been wholesome instead of vicious and seditious, could some seer penetrating the future with undoubted sagacity, have recognized the full meaning of the situation, the condition of both races would today be vastly different. Mistakes are often better seen through the retrospective than through the prospective.

Gradually front to front rose two generations of racial and opposing strangers, the one inheriting the assertion of rights guaranteed by the government, and remembering the troubles of the years of the immediate past with not a little of racial hatred; the other resisting such assertion, and disposed to take advantage directly or obliquely, and resolved to save the institutions of the South to the whites, there was nothing in a condition like this conducive to harmony, but everything to hostility.

The multiplied events of this second period were

portentous of much sad disorder and demoralization for which the immediate future stood in wait.
With these troubles the public is altogether too
familiar for them to be recounted here. New complications arose, collisions were frequent, and demoralization ensued. There is another fact generally
left out of account in presenting the elements which
entered into the period, and which the faithful chron-
icler would be remiss of duty should he fail to record
it. While the original slave holder and his descendants were in the main actuated by a sense of
pity for the recent and often misguided serf of other
days, he who owned not slaves, the whites on the
lower levels, were the inveterate enemies of the
Negro. Between the two, the thriftless whites and
the slaves, there had all along been a smothered
antipathy. It was as customary on the part of the
slave to respect a slave owner as it was to regard
with contempt those whom they called "po' white
trash." Mutual hatred characterized these two elements of Southern society. Seizing the occasion of
the Negro's crucial hour, these old-time enemies
became conspicuous in the wreak of vengeance, and
with no knowledge of the black man, other than that
he was a "nigger," many of this class of whites have
been demonstrative in their opposition to the progress of the Negro, and to his general welfare. While
this does not admit of universal application to this
class of whites, many there were, and still are, among
them who cherish hostility toward the Negro. In

the upheavals of fortune and misfortune which have come to the South in its era of transition, some of this class have come to more or less of conspicuousness, while by the same law of revolution many of the once wealthy and aristocratic of the South have receded in influence, because of the novelty of the bustling times, in consequence of both which conditions the Negro has been made to suffer.

Three distinct propositions were eventually evolved from the chaotic conditions following the close of the Civil War. One of these was that of the disposal of the Negro. That he was valuable as a laborer, and that he was the only available laborer for the plantations of the South, every land owner recognized. While he was not desired as a citizen, he was as a laborer. Citizen or not, he must be retained to cultivate the soil, for which he was admirably adapted and for which he had been trained and tried. The muscle of the Negro had much to do with saving him from sorer troubles than those which he had to undergo. That fact conjoined with a sense of protection in the breast of many a Southerner interposed in his behalf.

Another proposition was that of adopting such a course of humanity as to be considerate of the claims due the Negro, and, at the same time, preserve the well-being of society. While there were those, and still are, who oppose his intellectual advancement, there was a preponderance of Southern sentiment which favored it, else the Negro would never have had a school, for the old threadbare tradition has not ceased to prevail with a certain class in the South, that education would mean the Negro's undoing.

A third proposition had respect to the general healthfulness of the tone of the American nation, and such an adjustment of the new order as would bring to pass that condition. In the very nature of the case, the nation is to be more or less affected by the outcome of the Negro question. Tasks like these were the ones to which the sage wisdom of the states of the South set itself. As time has passed, the situation has been one between repression on the one hand, and of construction on the other. To repress the Negro and deny him the most ordinary rights, even the right of working for a livelihood excepting under servile conditions, represents one element of Southern sentiment; to rehabilitate and construct a new system, one adjusted to the demands of existing conditions, leaving the Negro untrammelled to shape the destiny of his numerous and growing race, in a region in which he is an undoubted fixture, is representative of another sentiment of the South.

Meanwhile the Negro, himself, has not been inactive in contributing to the solution of the difficulty and in affording omens which serve in no small way to brighten the future. To the surprise of all, even of his most expectant and sanguine friends, he has produced a leadership of great and surprising worth. Ambitious and worthy spirits even from the stripling class of young slaves, possessed of foresight, prudence, wisdom, and the hardier virtues, have met the shock of disadvantage under which the race was left by the turbulence of years, and with a display of manhood which has challenged the admiration of all, have vindicated their worth by the stations which they have made for themselves and in honor of their race.

As from ignorance they have attained to scholarship; from penury to competence, and even to fortune; from a vagabondism where slavery left them, when they were released from its bonds, to the erection of good homes and to the ownership of lands, and from the gross conditions of immorality to those of respectability and honor, these leaders have become the harbingers of hope and of inspiration to the race, and have set forever at nought the opinions held in former years of the incapacity of the Negro to stand alone.

True, the croak is sometimes heard that the Negro has made no such progress as is justified by the privileges which he has so abundantly enjoyed. But it is charitable to suppose that those who now make such charge are not aware of the amazing strides which have been made. That the Negro has done so much, done it so marvellously well, and within so short a period of time, is creditable not only to him, but would be to any people similarly situated.

When it is remembered that two and a half centuries ago the ancestry of this race was savages in the land of the Dark Continent, and that forty-five years ago some of these same Negroes and their ancestors were slaves on the plantations of the South, it is astounding that they were able to enter the gateway of the new century with so many demonstrations of genuine progress. To claim, as is sometimes done, that no people of inherent worth would have submitted so willingly to the galling servitude of more than two hundred years, and to offer that in proof of their inherent weakness and worthlessness, is sufficiently answered by the historic fact that the Hebrew race, the most wonderful people of all time, was in servitude for four hundred years, was grossly ignorant when the bondage of slavery was broken, was embruted by slavery, was superstitious, and at the end of forty years was not sufficiently recovered from the dire effects of servitude to be entrusted to entrance into the land of promise.

To have seen the surging multitude of Hebrews, said to have been two million strong, on the border of the Red Sea, when the Egyptian host thundered threatingly in the rear, would have inspired but slight hope of the future prominence of the race; but within that ignorant mass lay the germ of the future church, the blessings of our Christianity, and the coming of the Son of God. They, too, produced but few leaders in the outset, but as a people they have spread the influence of their power around the habitable globe. Of course, the conditions attending the two races were vastly different. The Negro has within easy reach the facilities of advancement. But the comparative advantages are not the question involved, but that of the possibility of the Negro to make progress. If there was nothing in the Negro to respond, no inherent quality, no germ of prophecy, he could never have risen at all, and certainly not to the point to which he has surprisingly attained, when it is remembered that he has been compelled to contest every inch of the way against the gravest of disadvantages. Effort is making the Negro, as it invariably makes civilization. The Indian enjoyed the same advantage, but he decayed under the influence of civilized life.

Let it be remembered also that when one speaks of the advancement made, or not made, by the Negro, his standard of judgment is that of a race which for full eight hundred years, or more, has been pushing along the highway of progress. If a comparison be instituted, let it be between the African in Africa and the African in America, and not between the Anglo-Saxon with his growing culture of many centuries, and a race the birth-hour of whose freedom dates back to a period of less than fifty years. A race no more than an individual can change its habits and customs overnight.

These general statements bring the situation somewhat before us, and prepare us for a more specific presentation of that which is to follow.

CHAPTER II.

By the stereotyped expression, "The Negro Problem," is commonly understood that condition which has arisen in the states of the South since the close of the Civil War, and in consequence of the freedom of the Southern slave. That the "problem" came to its culmination at that time is true, but that it is a condition confined altogether to the brief period in which it reached its consummation, is not true. The roots of the trouble run back under two and a half centuries, and its incipiency was when the first slave ship set sail from the coasts of Africa. Its beginning was occasioned by the dealer in human souls as a commodity of traffic, and one in which the Negro himself had no part, save in an humble and passive way as an object of commerce. Born of the spirit of cupidity, it was nursed in the interest of gain, and when the Negro ceased to be a chattel it assumed the proportions for which it was logically destined when the first purchase of slaves was made in Africa.

Slavery under certain conditions was not new when the importation of Africans to America began. For ages a custom had prevailed among barbarous peoples to reduce to slavery prisoners cap-

tured in war, but this was only one of the methods
by which people were enslaved, for they were bought
and sold in divers ways from ancient times down to
the nineteenth century. For centuries together Africa had been a common slave market for different
nations. Prior to the discovery of America, the
Arabs had been the most active in the purchase of
slaves in Africa. While the African was bought by
themselves sometimes for traffic, the general use of
the slave was that of service or labor to the Arab
master. The discovery of the New World and the
subsequent development of the mines and plantations, which required severe toil, physical endurance,
and unusual hardship, gave a fresh impulse to the
African slave trade. By reason of these develop-
ments on a new continent, the value of the raw slave
was advanced, and the importation of Africans
quickened. If the discovery of America was an
immense blessing it was not unattended by as dire
a curse as ever afflicted humanity. It does not come
within the province of this work to enter at length
on a history of the slave trade, and only to allude to
it thus briefly because of its connection with the
matter now under consideration.

The Negro is in America, then, not because of
any volition of his own, but by reason of compulsion. Either by kidnapping or by purchase from
petty savage chiefs in Africa, he fell into the hands
of the American slave dealer, and was brought
hither and sold into servitude.

The lack of adaptation of the Negro slave to New England, on account alike of climatic conditions and the infertility of the soil, and the success of slave labor in Virginia from the founding of Jamestown onward, led to his gradual drift to the warmer states and the rich agricultural lands of the South. The rapid development of the South following the close of the war of 1812, and the increased peopling of the regions westward, created a growing demand for slaves with physical strength and power of endurance alike beneath the hot suns of the South and in regions infected by malaria, for which the white man was not prepared. The Negro, inured to conditions like these in his own tropical Africa, was therefore in great demand for this arduous service.

While the middle of the nineteenth century found the Negroes massed, for the most part, in the states of the South, from Maryland to Texas and Arkansas and Missouri, they had traveled all the way across the continent from New England. If Southern planters bought the slaves, Northern traders, in the earlier years, sold and supplied them. "If Charleston, South Carolina, was one of the chief ports of destination for slave-trading vessels, Salem, Massachusetts, was one of the chief ports from whence these vessels sailed."*

*Extract from an address of Hon. W. H. Fleming before the Alumni Society of the University of Georgia, June 19, 1906.

For generations, then, Southerners came naturally to regard the slave as a legitimate commodity in trade, and as a serf designated for just the labor which was imposed on him. His servitude was easy, his temper docile and tractable, and his labor was remunerative, especially on the fields of the further South. The slave himself, after the first generation had passed, ignorant of his origin, and knowing nothing of his ancestry, was disposed to regard his servitude as his natural destiny. His profit lay largely in his ignorance of the wherefore of his servitude, and most sedulously was he preserved in that ignorance by the white master. His prolificness was encouraged by every possible means, just as was that of the grazing herds of the owner, because his increase meant an enhancement of wealth. Laws were enacted in the slave states to hedge him about with ignorance, that he might not learn his real condition, and the virtue of chastity was a thing rarely known among Negroes. The birth of a slave child was hailed on the plantation as an additional accumulation of wealth, and it was a matter of slight importance how the issue came. From his earliest years, the Negro was trained into submission, and thence disciplined into perfect obedience. His rearing was amidst the exactions of hardship, and naturally and conditionally he was seasoned for hard and exacting service. There was not lacking the inculcation of certain destructive

vices by the examples of white men, whom the slave
reverenced and who were to the serf the highest
ideals of integrity. In some instances, rewards for
productiveness in child-bearing were offered on
Southern plantations, and but little was presented
as an encouragement to the virtue of chastity.
For centuries the utmost laxity as to morals prevailed on Southern plantations. Craven fear of
punishment was the prime motive to honesty and
truthfulness. If one was a successful thief he felt
that he was but getting a portion of his due, as he
was the creator of the wealth of the master.

In this deplorable condition, lasting through generations of the enslaved race, there were forecast
the horrors which were to come in the years of the
future. In the processes, step by step, beginning
with the capture of the Negro savage on his native
shores, and running through his experiences and
those of his descendants, was ripening the Negro
problem of the present.

While all this was going on, the moral sentiment
of the world against slavery was rising and bearing
with greater force against the system in the South.
The revolution was irresistible, and slavery was
doomed. Now and then, under the stress of the discussion which went on for years, a Southern master
would reach the conviction that human slavery was
wrong in principle, and would voluntarily manumit
his slaves.

Quite naturally the South was the last portion of

the country to which general attention was called with respect to slave liberation, because the Negroes were mainly massed on the rich lands of that region. Just as naturally the Southern owner was reluctant to relinquish his hold on his slaves because they were the most valuable of his possessions,—the basis of his industrial system, and of his commerce. Trained to regard his slaves as his rightful property, he was ready to defend his rights by biblical logic, by constitutional provision, and if need be, by the use of the bullet and the sword. His slaves were his by purchase or by inheritance, and from this conception the logic was easy to a position of defense of African servitude, based on the adaptation of the Negro as a laborer to the fields of the South. The torrid sun, the heavy and stubborn but fertile soils, so ill adapted to the labor of the tenderer white, the muscularity of the slave, his servile obedience, his cheerfulness in toil, his uncomplaining mood in the enjoyment of the scant comfort afforded, his devotion and loyalty to his master, and most of all, the beneficence of the system of slavery in comparison with the dismal conditions of mentality and utter absence of civilization of his fatherland—what more was needed to justify the perpetuation of African slavery?

But the principle of human freedom obtaining elsewhere over the world, found its way with increasing pressure into the states of the South. The world was moving and leaving in its wake the relics of barbarism of which slavery was one. Slavery was doomed.

Silently the forces of the race problem were converging toward a given point. While the Southern planter was complacently congratulating himself that he was being enriched by the multiplied progeny of his slaves, he was only increasing the complicated elements of the race question which was to loom into frowning prominence in the years of the future. His supposed blessing was, after all, not unalloyed. All supposed advantages of slavery were but hidden obstructions of the race question which had been on the march since first the wrong began by enforced slavery on the African coast. The problem was already growing toward maturity and consummation. In vain was the ethics of human liberty and of reciprocity openly repudiated in the schools and colleges of the South. When that portion of moral instruction was reached in the schools, counter lectures were delivered in defense of slavery as a biblical system, so blinded were the cultured people of the South by their valuable slave possessions and to its ultimate consequences. Given certain premises of choice, the argument will be forced to certain conclusions of satisfaction, even though it be wrong. Only Right lives and moves on a straight line into the light, while Wrong is blindfolded till retribution lifts the alarm, and the bandage is taken from the eyes. The brothers of Joseph did not realize so fully the wrong done, till it was disclosed in the perplexity encountered long years afterward in Egypt. "We are verily guilty concerning our brother, in that we saw the anguish of his soul, when he besought us, and we would not hear; therefore is this distress come upon us."

Never were a people sincerer, never a cause more manfully struggled for, than the cause of African serviture by strong and able men of the South. Every scrap of defense in behalf of the institution of slavery was adduced. To mock their efforts even at this late day were unbecoming, but it seems strange that with an inception such as domestic servitude had, in human piracy and in corrupt dicker, there should not have been an occasional misgiving of the righteousness of the cause so ardently defended. The wrong done at the fountain source could not clear the stream of its sediment however brilliant the injected rhetoric, however keen the incisive logic. A wrong begun and prosecuted works itself out to its conclusion, however sinuous its course, and however it may be sought to be averted.

The race problem, considering it in its full scope as embracing the period of the regime of slavery, was not unattended by certain advantages, some of which fell to the lot of the slave himself, but that does not atone for the original wrong done. To kidnap, decoy, purchase, or otherwise get possession of the African on his own distant shores was either right or wrong. If right, it should have been done, and all the defense of slavery was correct.

But to insist on its rightness would be subversive
of the code of morals. If wrong, then no amount
of kindness done the slave, no reasoning however
able, no views however sincere, can displace the
wrong done. The slave dealer, then, as the prime
origin of Negro servitude, was also the primitive
source of the much-mooted race problem. *If* the
Negro had been left in Africa, the race problem
would not be. Why is he here? How came he
here? These questions answered, answers also the
question of the origin of the race problem.

Had the Negro been a foreign immigrant in the
sense in which others are who have sought our
shores from preference; had he come as have come
the Irishman, German, Italian, Japanese, Chinese,
and all the rest, and had he under conditions like
these been the occasion of existing complications,
then it would be not only the Negro problem, but
the problem of the Negro. But he was forcibly
seized, or otherwise gotten forcible possession of,
and by that same force brought to America, injected into American life with all the possible complications attaching to his presence—not complications
of his own making, but those of the whites, who
have manipulated, swayed, directed, and controlled
his course every step of the way, from the landing
of the slave ships more than two hundred and fifty
years ago to the present. By a partnership of the
self-seeking purchaser and owner of the slave, and
of all others connected with him, and the direction

of affairs of a mysterious Providence, the so-called race problem has come to its logical consummation. No matter how it has been brought about, the responsibility of such result rests not on the Negro, but on the white man. The Negro has been only a passive agent, a subjective instrument, and in nothing that has occurred in his history has he been the prime mover, and is therefore not responsible. He did not leave Africa by volition, he did not voluntarily assume the function of servitude, he did not emancipate or enfranchise himself, he did not draft the amendments to the national constitution adopted in his behalf—he did none of these things, but they were the work of the whites. The result is therefore not chargeable to the Negro, nor is the problem his. In order to find the source of the trouble which we popularly call the Negro problem, we must follow up the stream two hundred and fifty years, and seek its source in the land of Ham. Sheer fairness demands that we visit not on the Negro, because he is a Negro, the consequences of a train of events, nor of their resultant, when he has had nothing whatever to do either in setting them in motion or in directing them. As well might the pilot burn his boat for striking a snag in the stream when he himself was in the pilot house.

This seems a primary principle necessary of recognition before we are prepared to take the first step toward the solution of the race question. It is historic as a fact, and just as a moral principle. Because of the benefits derived as a result of Negro labor for more than two and a half centuries, not by a few only, not only by the owners of slaves, but by all alike, of all sections of the country, the white race is committed as a whole and morally, to afford proper relief to the present situation, in a way reputable to the white man and equitable to the black.   .

CHAPTER III.

At this juncture of the discussion it is not inappropriate, in the light of the facts involved in the great race question, to call attention to the suggestions of providence concerning the outcome of the history of the African-American, for as a Christian nation, dealing with a problem of anomalous character and of vast proportions, and one, too, which vitally concerns our entire American life, we cannot well leave this phase of the question out of account.

Brought to America, as the Negro was, by coercion, and reduced to slavery for a long period of time, and denied most of the ordinary rights of humanity, with no will, judgment, or conscience, save that derived from a dominating power, the sole aim of which was financial profit—a race which in the evolution of Providence finally emerged into freedom with all that that nominally means in a democracy, and yet the victim of much injustice, is there nothing in all this to appeal to the American conscience? That there is much in the varying phases of Negro history in America to suggest the direct agency of a guiding Providence seems unquestionable.

Impelled by a lust for profit, and regardless of
all else in the enforced subordination of millions of
an unoffending race, the stronger race now finds
itself inextricably entangled in a network of conditions from which there is, at present, no visible
means of escape. Meanwhile the released race with
dramatic pathos and with uncherished passion of
unkindness for all past wrong—the shuttle in the
loom of contention between two mighty sections of
the white strength, struggles on uncontrolled by the
thoughts of the past, and unbaffled by the disadvantages of the present, to gain a foothold of hopefulness. In this hubbub of confusion and contention, the Negro produces no discord by undue claim,
but simply asks the recognition which is due a man
joining in the rough encounters of the world, and
for the chance of a livelihood along with other men.
Considering all this, is there not a suggestion of
equity to the American mind?

As a race, the Negro is unable to take the initia-
tive in the appeal of his cause to the stronger race.
Because of the strained relations between the two
races, white and black, and because of the subordinate position which he is forced to occupy, any ini-
tiative on his part would be regarded as imperti-
nent, and would therefore go unheeded. He must
needs, therefore, accept whatever is granted, and
await the favorable action of his white neighbor.
In all the transactions concerning himself he has

had no part nor lot, and is oblivious to the past, if only in the future he may be given a chance. The remarkable leadership developed by the race, despite the accumulated disadvantages encountered, asks for its people nothing more than an opportunity to demonstrate their merit. It asks not to be taken as a ward or regarded as a fondling, nor yet as a mendicant does it seek pity, but only that it may be able to stand full on its feet in the attitude of manliness. This is the reasonable request of the leaders of the race, the achievements of whom merit attention and excite confidence. In the face of the facts already briefly stated, in what condition do we now find this lately enslaved race? In the section which it served so long under the conditions already named and fully known, the Negro is hedged about by restrictions which often prevail in the denial of the simplest justice in the courts, his development is opposed by many, his rights to labor is in some instances denied, opposition is raised to his presence in some quarters, in most questions of popular contention between him and the stronger race the result is usually unfavorable to him, so that he is compelled often to scramble for a mere footing in the ordinary jobs of life.

In the criminal courts prejudice and passion rather than justice are often accorded him, and under the guise of a false chivalry and a monstrous perversion of law he is frequently taken and hanged

without the opportunity of a syllable of defense.
All that is wrong concerning him is paraded before
the world in such a way as to involve the whole race,
irrespective of merit or demerit, while his worthier
acts go unnoticed—the heroic efforts of thousands
of them to render aid and benevolent assistance to
yet other thousands on the inferior planes of life;
the daily industry of millions in domestic service,
on the fields, in the varied vocations of business, in
the schools, churches, and on the distant fields of
missionary endeavor; the Negro's ambition shown in
the purchase of lands from earnings eked from the
most exacting economy, in the establishment and
maintenance of libraries, in the founding of publishing houses, and in the establishment of good
homes—who knows of these things?

This is a plain, general statement of fact concerning the Negro in the states of the South, relieved, it
is cheerfully admitted, by certain exceptions of individual consideration in his behalf, but the facts,
as recorded, remain. Yet in the face of all these
conditions, conditions produced by the stronger and
dominating race, we speak of the Negro as an "undesirable citizen," a menace, a peril, and as the
occasion of an "impending crisis." Instead of consideration we often employ exasperation, and for
patience, more frequently than otherwise, substi-
tute passion. If, then, the condition today be one of
strained relations and of unfortunate misunder-

standings between the two races, is the Negro
wholly responsible?

The facts above recorded relate to conditions in
the South, and yet despite these, the Negro finds
ampler scope and bigger opportunity here than he
does elsewhere. Not that this last statement in the
least impairs the integrity of those already made,
but serves the rather to show the grave disadvantages of the Negro in a country for which he has
done so much, and for which he was almost wholly
unrequited.

Without sectional or partisan bias, and prompted
alone by the desire to get before us facts, how about
the treatment of the Negro at the North? On this
subject Professor N. S. Shaler, of Harvard University, has recently spoken with authoritative emphasis, and declares that racial antipathy is as deep
toward the Negro at the North as elsewhere. It
would seem from his statements that certain barriers are raised in the way of the Negro in the
North, as certain other obstructions are thrown in
his way in the South. In the North the Negro is
denied membership in the labor-unions, and then in
order to seal hermetically the situation against him,
an employer is forbidden to engage the services of
non-union labor. In other words, the Negro is pre-
cluded altogether. Should the employer engage the
services of Negroes, the members of the labor
unions, rather than work beside the colored men,

decline to labor at all. Besides these, it is a fact well known, that even in some of the menial functions of industry, the Negro is denied employment, purely on account of color. This pertains to certain hotels, restaurants, barber shops, and to domestic service as hostlers, butlers, maids, janitors, sextons, and other similar functions.

In the North the Negro can ride with the whites in street cars and on railway trains, which privilege is denied him in the South; he can occupy a place, along with the whites, in the schools, churches, and operas in the North, but not in the South—almost any thing which may involve the payment of money, he can have North, but not South. In the South he does find opportunity to make a dollar; in the North he is given opportunity to spend it. This is only putting in another form the language of Dr. Booker T. Washington, when he says, "If the Negro would spend a dollar at the opera, he will find the fairest opportunity at the North; if he would earn the dollar, his fairest opportunity is at the South. The opportunity to earn his dollar fairly is of much more importance to the Negro just now, than the opportunity to spend it at the opera."

Again, this greatest of Negro leaders says, "It is at the South that the black man finds an open sesame in labor, industry and business that is not surpassed anywhere. It is here that that form of slavery which prevents a man from selling his labor to whom he pleases on account of his color, is almost unknown. We have had slavery in the South, now dead, that forced an individual to labor without a salary, but none that compelled a man in idleness while his family starved."

Yet, in the South, as has already been shown, and as is well known, there are certain restrictions imposed, and privileges denied, even in the field of industry sometimes, because of color. There are many simple features of justice denied the Negro, which could be accorded without hurt or compromise, and yet which are withheld because of a dark skin. Without captiousness this is written respecting the treatment of the Negro in both regions, North and South.

Toward what does all this tend? Toward the creation of a condition throughout the Union of an economic disturbance even to irritation—a perpetual restlessness that necessarily throws conditions out of poise. If this condition shall continue to prevail, that which we now account a problem, will become mere child's play in the complications which the future is destined to bring. It boots but little to create conditions such as have been described, and then lift our hands in holy horror and say, "How can we solve the problem?" It is of small worth to write learned essays on social and economic conditions with a certain tang of dismay, when the root of the conditions lies untouched. It is not necessary to become frantic or extravagant about the Negro, and to seek to enlarge his importance—that is not the matter at issue—it is a fundamental principle as plain in the code of ethics as the sun in the heavens.   *I*t is a principle that strikes at the basis of a nation which has a heterogenous and cosmopolitan population.   To hedge, deny, repress and oppress, by means of sheer force will inevitably produce a condition through which justice will inevitably break as certainly as God reigns.   The slumber of justice is not its death.   That there is a power overruling and directing the destiny of the affairs of the world, a power transcending our plans, purposes and schemes, the history of every race and nation teaches.

History records only the footprints of Providence, and in the sudden transitions which have frequently taken place, there are seen so many revolutions of the wheel which is guided by an unseen Hand. Force may prevail for a period, arrogance may hold sway for a season, and wrong may seem triumphant; but they are moving under a directing Hand, not in the interest of a race or a people merely, but in the interest of principle which must be finally uppermost.   At some point in the future, though long delayed it may be, in order to accomplishment, that purpose will be revealed.

The iniquity of the system of slavery has wrought and still works.   That wrong principle abides yet in American life.   Nothing is gained by an effort to resist an inexorable law.   It works unseen, works with silent force, and transmutes the plans, the schemes and the acts of men into agents in the consummation of its ultimate result. They are bewildering—the examples and illustrations of history in proof of this statement. A course of wrong, a policy of injustice can never reach the result of right.

As applied to the present discussion, it is easy to say that this is "negrophobia," and to denounce one as a "negrophile," but that answers nothing. When a given policy or course can portend nothing less than peril alike to justice and to freedom, it were criminal to be silent. There is nothing novel or unusual in the enunciation of certain homely ethical principles. They are as old as the race, and are written on every page of human history. Nor have such enunciations been without utterance from Southern sources even within recent years. In 1903, said the Montgomery (Ala.) Advertiser: "The white race has a duty which is imperative. It is a duty which is demanded by justice, by humanity, and by self interest. Ours is and will ever be the governing race. It will elect the lawmakers, make the laws, and enforce them. That being so, that principle of eternal justice which bids the strong protect the weak, makes it our duty to protect the Negro in all his legal, industrial and social rights. We should see that he has equal and exact justice in the courts, that the laws bear alike on the black and the white, that he be paid for his labor just as the white man is paid, and that no advantage be taken of his ignorance and credulity. . . . . .

"And the task is a simple and easy one. The courts and juries should know no difference between whites and blacks, when a question of right and justice is up for settlement. The man who employs a Negro to work for him should deal as fairly with him as he would deal by a white man. The life of a Negro who has done no wrong should be as sacred as the life of a white man. He is in our power, politically and otherwise, and justice, humanity, and good policy unite in demanding for him an equal and exact justice. Keep the Negroes among us, give them the full protection of the laws, and let them have justice in all things. That is the solution of the race problem."*

"Careless seems the great Avenger; history's pages but record
One death grapple in the darkness, 'twixt old systems and the World;
Truth forever on the scaffold, Wrong forever on the throne—
Yet the scaffold sways the future, and, behind the dim unknown,
Standeth God within the shadow, keeping watch above his own."

Nor is this sentiment exceptional in the states of the South. There is much robust sentiment of the same character throughout the better element of Southern people. Still, conditions heretofore described, prevail. It may be idle for the time to

*Quoted from a footnote in Murphy's "The Present South," pp. 182-3.

protest against them, but they as certainly bear within themselves the germs of retributive justice as that the stars shine.

There is a higher law than that of human will, whether it be expressed in the force of practical action, or on the statute books of the commonwealth. This higher law has ultimately prevailed in the moral government of the world in the past, and will continue to do so in the future.

CHAPTER IV.

THE SOUTHERN NEGRO AS HE IS.

To have the Negro before us as fully as possible, not in an abstract way, but concretely, and to be able to see him and know him, as he is, will prove of great value as we shall consider him in the subsequent chapters of this work. That there is prevalent much misunderstanding and the absence of accurate information respecting the Negro, will be readily admitted. It must also be admitted that there is much prejudice in the public mind of the white race concerning the Negro, so that in some instances the mere mention of the subject is sufficient to awaken prejudice, which is an invariable barrier to all right thinking, and, of course, to any satisfactory conclusion. By divesting our minds of prejudice or of any notions which have hitherto controlled us in our estimate of the Negro, and by a faithful study of him, as he actually exists in the states of the South, we shall no doubt find it a matter of profit alike to ourselves and to the Negro race. Of his natural disposition, his temper, and his dominant characteristics we shall have occasion hereafter in these pages to speak. What now concerns us is the classification of the Negroes of the South.

Naturally there were diversities and differences which were recognized among the Negroes even while they were slaves on the plantations of the South. There were subordinate leaders developed, so far as the system of slavery allowed development, and developed to a point where the spirit of leadership was inexorably checked, but leadership nevertheless there was, which differentiated the inferior from the superior. To such leaders on the plantations was accorded certain discretion in the direction of affairs in a subordinate way, and such leaders were usually called "drivers." The limitation of authority with which they were entrusted differed widely on different plantations. The duty of the "driver" was to superintend or direct the performance of a certain portion of work assigned to him and his "gang" apart from others, for the proper execution of which he was responsible, of all of which minor distinction the slave was duly proud. There was an instance of which the present writer knew in the "Black Belt" of Alabama, where a slave of established reputation, having grown old, was made by his master a sort of arbiter in the adjudication of differences between slaves, and even of those between the slaves and the white overseer, or superintendent, during the absence of the owner. This old man was exempt from all labor and was charged alone with the function already named. Thus even in slavery there was not unrecognized that superiority among Negroes which found expression in the

general leadership of that race when the Negro
entered on his career in the new orbit of freedom.
In view of these facts it is the less surprising that
we find the widely differing classes in the race today. In certain particulars, the lines of separation
are very distinct. Any failure to recognize this distinction by the exercise of judgment concerning the
entire race based on the crimes of the few, is exceedingly unjust, and acts as a serious barrier to the
progress of the Negro race, and indirectly levels a
blow at the welfare of all the people, for to affect
one portion is to affect all. As Edmund Burke long
ago expressed it, we cannot indict a whole people,
neither can we hold a race responsible for the deeds
of the few. It is most unfortunate, certainly at this
particular juncture, that the Negro is the only race
that is so judged. If a crime be committed by any
other than a Negro, it is the individual that is recognized; if committed by a Negro, the entire race is
implicated. This has been the occasion of much
unnecessary friction, of much ill-advised judgment.
Not till the lines of cleavage are justly drawn in the
distinction between the different classes of Negroes
will there come a proper accord of desert to those
whose every energy is being bent toward the accomplishment of the most for their people and for the
good of the American people at large. Far more
than is commonly known are the Negroes of the
higher types doing what they can for the elevation
of those who move on the lower levels. With the

proper accord of merit there will result a corresponding progress in the solution of the race question in the states of the South.

The Negro race of the South may be said to be divided into three classes—the intelligent leaders, the large middle or laboring class, and the criminal class. The highest class is not so large as that of the middle class, and yet it is larger than that of the lowest or criminal class. That highest class is constantly increasing in numbers, while there is a perceptible decrease in the lowest class. While accessions to the ranks of the highest class come from the middle class, both the upper and middle classes, by a combined influence for good, are tending to relieve the lowest class. Of the forces daily at work in this direction, the public is commonly unaware. Any word spoken to the detriment of the race, any unwarranted action taken by the stronger race, acts as a hindrance and handicap to a people, the efforts of whom for the good of their own people have never been anywhere surpassed. It is hoped that this will be demonstrated in the subsequent pages of this work.

Emerging from the great mass of ignorance which characterized the Negro race in the dawn of emancipation there were certain leaders among the Negroes who came to be recognized among their people as such, a number small at first, but of sufficient strength to gain the attention of the race. With wise discrimination and quiet judgment these leaders foresaw the necessity first of becoming exemplars to their people at a time when irritation was fresh and sensitive at the South, in the establishment of the maintenance of those principles without which the race must ever remain in a condition more or less degraded. Never was an undertaking more difficult, never was one attended by more serious disadvantage, and it may be said, never was there more genuine pluck exhibited than was shown by these same projectors on a basis on which their lately enslaved people might be able to come to a position of respectability and usefulness in the American republic.

These leaders had themselves been slaves, and they knew the temper of the great white race, and with the spirit of adjustability for which the Negro is remarkable, and without which he would have gone as has gone the *I*ndian, they entered as pioneers on what seemed a forlorn hope. Quietly availing themselves of whatever facilities lay within their reach for equipping themselves for usefulness, they have steadily held on their course, blazing the way for the great mass to follow. As they have pressed up the heights, inch by inch, they have been a source of inspiration to the millions below. Eager in the pursuit of knowledge, none ever turned to more practical account the slender resources within reach, none ever made more crucial sacrifice. The intrinsic value of this class of men to the country at large, even though they are Negroes, has never been fully appreciated by the American people. They were the first to find a path out of the tangled wilderness produced by the chaos which followed the period of emancipation, for none of which were they responsible. The exploits of these people in a realm of their own creation have done more to relieve the difficulties attendant on the race question than is commonly supposed. These leaders have never been arrogant, never presumptuous, never turbulent or self-assertive against the white race, but always patient, always respectful, and their influence on their own race has been potent for good beyond measure. It is a remarkable fact that a Negro leader amounts to more and accounts for more among his own people than does that of a leader among any other people. That these initial leaders with such clearness of discrimination seized on this fact to turn it to so vast advantage reflects on them immense credit. Nothing could have been more timely for the Negro race, nothing for the good of the country at large, than that there arose such a class of leaders, at just such a juncture among the Negro masses of the South.

Without a leadership like this, it is impossible to say what the results would have been. These same leaders, naturally endowed as they were, had they become leaders in the opposite direction, would have been the occasion of horrible consequences throughout the States of the South. That they moved upward toward a higher sphere and for the best things attainable is a matter of exceeding great credit to themselves, and one that calls for the plaudit of every unbiased white citizen throughout the land. The achievements wrought in education, in professional life, in commerce, and in the establishment of the idea of homelife among their people, are in themselves considered, a vast benefaction to the country. And when we consider the influence wrought on the race of which they are the worthy representatives, these leaders are worthy of all praise. The Negro race is not unlike all others in the invaluableness and indispensableness of a leadership. Most fortunate is the Negro race of the South in having as its initial leaders men of so quiet, robust and sturdy worth. They have set the pace for the race, and have set it well. In this service these Negro leaders have done for the country at large that which they only could do. No others could have effected so much for the race of which they are members, no other course could have been so productive of quiet good to the country. Nor is this all. This same class of deserving men have had frequently to encounter the sorest trials and confront the gravest difficulties. They have been severely tested, and much of the work done has been of a delicate nature. Themselves reaching a high plane, they serve as a perpetual animation to those who are striving to follow, and every year there have been substantial reinforcements added to this vanguard of Negro progress.

The second or middle class is the yeomanry of

the Negro race. Though less favored than their brethren on the upper level, they are not a whit less worthy. They are the laboring class—the men and women of hard and horny hands, and of patient perseverance. They are plain, many of them being unable to read, and laborious. In point of merit they range from the point of approximation to the highest of their race, to that of contact with the lowest. They constitute a large bulk of the race. In its elements this class is far more varied than either of the others. In their efforts to improve their conditions, the members of this class are often beguiled into unwary purchases to their detriment. In a cabin one finds sometimes a costly piano or organ, purchased on the installment plan, at an exaggerated figure. Again, their humble homes, far in the interior, are often ornamented by showy lightning-rods, as these unsuspecting people have fallen victims to loquacious venders. One of the chief difficulties with this class, and one which operates to their injury, is that many of them are excellent spenders of their hard-earned means.

Their ambition is to elevate their children, for the education of whom they will toil and spend to the last limit. From this class comes the seed-corn of the race. From out this mass come the boys and girls of brightness who in some distant school achieve scholarship or develop business power, and this, in turn, serves as a stimulus to a multitude of others. Steadily this class of industrious blacks is improving, are buying small tracts of land, and are learning to husband with more care their limited resources. The most serious practical drawback of this class is its disposition to spend. It furnishes gullible victims to oily-tongued peddlers and shrewd clerks in rural stores. These people are often easily bewitched by the showy and tawdry, and lack that provident spirit of "laying up for a rainy day."

But they are the backbone of the industrial system of the South. Their parents never toiled harder as slaves than do hundreds of thousands of these on the fields of the South today. With respect to their resources, many of them are content "to make ends meet" at the close of the year. While they enrich others by their toil, many remain unchanged in their financial condition from year to year.

There is, however, a perceptible change for the better in some quarters of the South, due largely to two causes, one of which is the influence of those who occupy a racial station higher up in life. Now and then representatives of this more favored class penetrate these masses, as genuine missionaries, and inculcate principles of thrift and economy by means of which the yeoman class is vastly aided. Another agency is that of the rural free delivery which brings these people into touch with the outside world. With increasing volume, books, papers, and magazines are finding their way into the far-off homes of these people. These serve to push back contracted horizons and awaken new visions of life. From this middle station there pass many each year into the higher class of Negroes. This constant reinforcement, going quietly on, gives increasing hopefulness to the future of the race. If the leaders find difficulty in clearing the way for the race to follow, those of the middle class find peculiar difficulty in maintaining their footing. In the centers of population much relief has come through the agency of savings banks, which the more progressive of the race are increasingly founding. Throughout the country the Negroes have well-nigh fifty such institutions which belong to the members of the race and are conducted entirely by them.

The last class to be noticed is that of the thriftless and criminal. The representatives of this class are the hangers-on about the suburban tenements of the towns and cities where they are content to dwell in poverty and vice, and often in squalor. Their homes are often miserable abodes, the haunts of drinkers, of gamblers, and of cocaine fiends. Notwithstanding the drastic laws enacted to regulate the sale of these deadly drugs, there are not wanting men of the white race who sell them from their shelves to the ignorant blacks. Of the inroads made by cocaine on these unfortunate people, through the agency of the conscienceless whites, there is but little known save by the investigator of conditions like these, and the police force. So much for those who infest the populous centers.

This criminal class is found also in the logging

camps, the mining regions, and on the far interior plantations of the South. It acts as a serious hindrance to the lower layer of the great middle class. Brought into frequent touch with this middle class, the contact is necessarily contaminating. Not infrequently in the milling regions of the South, this last class dwells apart from all others, in a segregated camp of tents, or huts, where the worst possible vices are practiced, and where these men are often boisterous and dangerous. From this class come the criminals of the race. The influence of its members is deadly wherever it touches the young of any other class. In these segregated retreats, or camps, these desperate Negroes are often a terror to the officers of the law. To invade these places is often to take one's life into his own hands. Fortunately this is quite a small percentage of the race, but its deeds are often heralded in such way through the press of the country as to imply that the criminals are the fit representatives of the entire race of which they happen to be members. Care is thus taken to draw the line of cleavage between the several classes of Negroes, and to indicate their characteristics, that they may not be confounded the one with the other. With this faithful classification one need not err with respect either to the worthiness or the unworthiness of the different classes into which the Negro race of the South is divided.

CHAPTER V.

In order to a candid consideration of this question one will have to bring to it a divestment of all preconceived notions unfavorable to the Negro as well as an abeyance of prejudice. Either we are debtors to the Negro or we are not. If so, how, why, and to what degree? If there be a debt is it one of humanity, or an obligation springing from gratitude, or one involving legitimate compensation? If there be the possibility of obligation, is it not proper that we seek to find it, and if discovered, to seek just as diligently to meet it? It is not insisted on in the outset that such obligation exists, but the bare possibility of it invites investigation. To this investigation let us now proceed.

It is not denied that, from existing conditions and from the relations between the white and black races in the South, there is prejudice and even repulsion oftentimes on the part of the whites. Much to the disadvantage of the Negro in his relations to the whites, he is oftener than otherwise seen at his worst. This is the side of the race oftenest held to the gaze of the world. The slovenly loiterer

along the streets, the denizens of the forbidding
haunts of the city suburbs, the rough laborer, worthy
or industrious though he may be, but clad in the
garb of the workman alike on the streets and on the
field, the court room with its herd of violators, the
cell with its inmates, the chain-gang on the streets,
or the occupant in stripes on the penal plantation or
in the workshop of the penitentiary, and the domestic servant not always honest in the manipulation of
the groceries, these conditions represent the race to
the eye of the public, and furnish the basis of the
popular estimate of the Negro race. In consequence,
it is more commonly understood than is generally
supposed that worth among Negroes is a rare quality, and that honor and honesty are the exceptions.
And yet the fact remains that there are thousands
among those, especially of the servants in the homes,
who are scrupulously honest and entirely trust-
worthy. This, I think, is a fair statement of the
case as it generally prevails.

The writers of articles on the Negro for enter-
prising journals from without the South, as well as
those on quaint and facetious characteristics from
within the South, present not the laudable side of
the Negro, because that is rarely turned to the eye
of the public. The descriptions often given are
much like that of the cocoanut as a fruit from a
description of the outside. We revert to a subject
already in part discussed in a previous chapter by
raising the question of the occasion of the presence

of the Negro in America. He is not here by any volition of his own, but by coercion; he was reduced to slavery which extended over a period of more than two and a half centuries; he labored with a loyalty and faithfulness unexcelled by any people in similar servitude; he felled our virgin forests, and transmuted them into plantations of beauty and profit; he built our homes, and was the means of the education of seven generations of Southerners; he furnished the means for the establishment of our commerce; he was for centuries the industrial system of the states of the South; he built the ships which floated at our wharves and which bore our products to distant parts; he laid our railway lines; he filled our coffers with gold for two hundred and more years; he furnished the means for the maintenance of a number of wars, and so far as the people of the South are concerned, he sustained the armies of the Confederacy during the great Civil War; he was the guardian of the helpless women and children of the South while the husbands and sons were at the distant front doing battle to preserve the shackles of servitude on his limbs; against him was not a whisper of unfaithfulness or of disloyalty during all this trying and bloody period; when the land was invaded by the armies which sought his freedom, he remained faithful still, and often at great personal risk of life, secreted from the invader the horses and mules, and buried the treasures of the family that they might not fall into the hands of the enemies of the whites, but the friends of the slave himself; in many thousands of instances he declined to accept freedom when it was offered by the invading army, preferring to remain loyal and steadfast to the charge committed to him by the absent master, all this and more the Negro slave did. There was not a day during the trying period of the Civil War when he might not have disbanded the Southern armies. An outbreak on his part against the defenseless homes of the South would have occasioned the utter dissolution of the Southern armies, and turned the anxious faces of the veterans in gray toward their homes. But no Southern soldier ever dreamed of the possibility of a condition like this. So far as his home was concerned, it was not any apprehension of the unfaithfulness of the slaves which occasioned the slightest alarm.

What other people known in history ever behaved with similar conduct? Where was ever anomaly like this? There was not wanting on the part of the slaves a knowledge of the occasion of the war. There were scarcely any who did not know what was involved in the conflict so far as they were concerned. Yet, there was this devotion which bound these faithful people to their masters. History is without a parallel of conduct like this.

Nor is this all. When the armies of the South capitulated and freedom came with suddenness to the Southern slave, did he assert his right to any portion of the property of which he was the chief

creator? Did he set up a claim which would have
been the occasion of fresh disorder to the Southern
soldier on his return to his home in his tattered
jacket of grey? So far from that being true, many
thousands of the recently enslaved cordially joined
the family of the returning veteran in affectionate
greeting when he finally reached his home. Not
a syllable of demand, not a murmur was heard from
the lips of the millions of the recently enslaved. On
the other hand, many thousands readily joined in
the endeavor to save the growing crops in the event-
ful spring of 1865, and as much to the Negro as to
any other is the country indebted that there was
not dire want entailed in consequence of the war,
which would have been in addition to the disastrous
effects of the conflict.

Let us suppose that a people other than the Negro
had rendered the same service as that rendered by
the slave during the war. Let us suppose that millions of Chinese or of Japanese had cultivated the
crops, protected the families of the absent soldiers,
fed and clothed the armies for a period of four years,
would there be any bound to our gratitude for the
service thus rendered? Poets would have extolled
them in song, and historians would have embalmed
them in extravagant praise, and our cities would
have been adorned with monuments of gratitude to
a people so loyal and devoted to our interests. When
LaFayette with a handful of Frenchmen came across
the Atlantic to assist in the achievement of American

independence the gratitude of the people knew no bounds, and our historic pages are still laden with expressions of laudation to the disinterested French. *I*s less due the Negro, especially since he came to America not of his own will, but was forced to our shores and reduced to slavery for a period covering seven generations of the history of his people?

Still further, the Negro was turned loose at the period of his emancipation without a penny in his pocket, without a loaf of bread, and without a shelter over his head. He had not a barleycorn of land, nothing which he could call his own but his muscle and will. He had enriched the states of the South with the cotton bale for many generations, he had equally enriched New England and the Middle States by the same means, and even while the hubbub of abolitionism was rampant, he was the chief means of the enrichment of the land, and what was the compensation afforded him? He was usually given a miserable hut in which to live; the scantiest clothing, of the coarsest sort; he was maintained on a peck of corn meal and three pounds of bacon a week; he was denied any rights save those of the scantiest nature; he was forbidden intellectual development, as that would have unfitted him for the profitable servitude to which he was subjected; he knew but little of the tender relationship of home life, as families were frequently sundered in the ordinary traffic of slaves as common property; he knew nothing but to labor from day to day, and from year to year, till he found his last resting place in the humble grave, into which a stream of seven generations of slaves passed before the boon of freedom came.

But it is claimed that slavery was a blessing in disguise to the imported African, as by that means he came into the possession of the dominant language of the globe, was taught the arts of industry, and was made a sharer in the benefits of the most splendid civilization the world has ever known. There is much plausible glamor in all this, but is there as much in it for the Negro as is ordinarily assumed? Of what use were all these if they could not be employed for his benefit? Whatever there was to him was merely incidental. If the character of the Negro was not benefited was there any genuine benefit at all? As Mark Hopkins says, "Man may have strength of character only as he is capable of controlling his faculties; of choosing a rational end; and, in its pursuit of holding fast to his integrity against all the might of external nature." Apply this principle to the Negro in his slavery, and what becomes of the much-boasted benefit of which we hear so much? The simple fact of slavery itself neutralized all the so-called benefit. It is not necessary to go into details of the influence of the dominating race on the race of slaves. The fact is well known that the animalism of the white owner and of others was not conducive to the highest ideals of character and of life. To the Negro slave the white owner was the ideal of manhood. He must needs learn from his conduct what life really is. How much was there in the conduct of the whites oftentimes to contribute to the erection of lofty character on the part of the Negro?

At its best estate, slavery was degrading and imbruting. The incidental advantages came far short of atoning for that of which the Negro was the compelled recipient. Entering on life for himself he had but little to take with him into his untried sphere. Certainly he had nothing whatever of this world's goods. For the incidental advantages for which so much is claimed, the Negro is indebted more to Providence than to man. These slight advantages happened to be inseparable from the degradation to which he was subjected. The motive of the slave owner generally was that of making the greatest number of dollars out of slavish labor, and not that of benefiting the Negro morally or otherwise. This is a plain statement of fact, and the fact speaks for itself.

Now, in view of this array of facts, the service of the slave for seven generations; the lack of compensation during that long period; the repression to which he was subjected; the devotion to the cause of the whites, a devotion unequalled in all history; the enrichment of the states by his labor; the fact that he was turned loose without a dime in his pocket, ignorant and defenseless in the presence of the machinations of evil men, is there nothing to suggest gratitude in all this? Is there nothing that appeals to the heart and conscience in his struggles to disinthrall himself from the conditions in which he finds himself? After all that can be said against the Negro, after the last word is spoken, the facts, as here presented remain, remain uncontested in their verity, and outweigh all that may be said to the contrary. Is there not due him in his struggles for a higher life at least the stimulation of encouraging words, and not the constant disposition to decry him? In spite of his original ignorance, his dire poverty, the denial of many of the primary rights due humanity, and the fiercest competition ever encountered by any people, he has mastered many of these, and by dint of genuine merit has evoked the admiration of the world.

With rapid strides the Negro has overcome the dismal illiteracy with which he was originally laden, so that of the ten million which now are, there are six million of them who have risen above illiteracy. Overcoming poverty, the Negro has bought lands, equipped plantations, built many excellent homes, established schools, erected churches, founded places of business, and is moving on the upgrade to higher and better things. Even though the Negro had remained in the leaden torpor of ignorance where emancipation found him, there would still be the obligation to assist him when by virtue of an excellence rarely shown by a lately enslaved race, he has accomplished so much, and is still pushing along the plane of achievement.

But the claim is common that the Negro is base, worthless, unreliable, and criminal. These epithets are quoted because they are of frequent occurrence, and are popular in their application to the Negro. Grant that all is true, does that forfeit our obligation to the race which has done so much for us? But these terms so glibly levelled against the Negro are not borne out by the facts in the case, as has been shown in a preceding chapter. Some of these may admit of application to some Negroes, but certainly not to the race, and to only a minor portion of the race. But, admitting that they be true, could not the same thing have been urged against the Cubans when our land enlisted in their behalf against Spain? *I*t is certainly true of many *I*talians, yet there was unstinted beneficence exhibited to that people when the disaster at Messina came. It is true of every nation to which the Christian churches send missionaries, and yet nobody hears all this assigned as a reason why we should withhold missionary aid from the benighted. On the contrary, this is assigned as the chief reason why help should be afforded the nations which sit in darkness. Why then should the American Negro, who has done so much for us, be made an exception? Must we, because of traditional prejudice against the Negro, a prejudice oftener unfounded than otherwise, deny him the aid which we can afford? Shall we suffer ourselves to be betrayed into the inconsistent attitude of withholding from the Negro the aid needed on the very grounds which furnish the most substantial basis for assistance?

We are debtors to the Negro, then, first of all, because of his willing and obedient servitude; because of his unrequited labors in the enrichment of the country; because of the services which he has substantially and effectively rendered to our American civilization; because of his loyalty and devotion, so far as the South is concerned, to her armies, her cause, and the families of the soldiery, and because of his efforts to rise in the scale of manhood in the face of unexampled obstructions.

Laying aside all preconceived ideas of the Negro, is there nothing due him? Dominated by a sense of justice and gratitude, as we should be, is there nothing to be accorded him? We find in him oftentimes an object of merriment, and laugh at his weird superstitions and his folklore, and.relish with a gusto the ignorance of the ignorant among them. We mete out to him the heaviest penalties in our courts, sometimes without justice, and fill our jails and penitentiaries with his race. He shares not in the courts, excepting as a criminal, has no place on the jury, though his cause is oftenest adjudicated, and in many instances we suffer him to undergo wrong and oppression because he is a Negro. He is denied in many instances, any trial at all, and miscreant officials sometimes suffer him to fall into the hands of violent men that they may wreak on him their vengeance. In his extremity we suffer him to live in a congested population on the outskirts of our cities, where he festers society with abhorrent vice. We permit the drinking den to demoralize and debauch his race by the ten thousand, or to use him for the clandestine sale of liquor, and the matter goes no further than to excite unfavorable comment against the Negro himself.

It is easy to denounce the low Negro, to threaten and hang him, but in a country of Christians is there not something else that may be done? Is it not due him from the point of view of humanity that more be done in his moral behalf? Aid is withheld from the millions because of the criminality of the few. It is here insisted, and must ever be, that the criminal be duly punished for his deeds, but is it not better to prevent the perpetration of crime by proper measures, than to punish the offender after the crime is committed?

It would seem in a great Christian land that there are some measures that might be adopted for the improved moral condition of the race, and not that it be permitted to suffer the utmost corruption without the slightest interposition on the part of Christian men and women. There are thousands of men and women among themselves who are seeking by every possible means to relieve their fallen ones, and that work is worthy of supplement at the hands of the best whites. It is not denied that in a limited way some do aid those of the Negro race who are seeking to bring relief where it is most needed; but while not abating one jot or tittle of the execution of the law, the gospel is a far more wholesome dissolvent of wrong-doing than the law. Is prejudice a stronger principle with us than piety? *If* the Negro be discounted because he is a Negro, we should remember our debt of gratitude to him because of the long services of the past. It would seem that the American people could never get out of sight of this obligation. His services were invaluable for centuries, and when he was no longer our chattel, we discard him as the offscouring of the earth. There is a debt which we owe him, whether we recognize it or not.

CHAPTER VI.

The Negro has been in America from the time of its first occupation by white colonies. For a period of more than two hundred and fifty years he was the slave of the whites, and seven generations of the slave race lie buried in the soil of the American states. The story of the African-American is one of toil, suffering, privation, and largely of unrequited labor. In all the revolutions, ruptures, and upheavals of our continental American life he has been a sharer. It is a noteworthy historical fact that the first blood spilt in the Revolution was that of Crispus Attucks, an intrepid Negro leader, and a slave, who when the British entered Boston, headed a party of whites and blacks, using stones, clubs, and even their clenched fists in resisting the invasion. Raising the cry that the way to drive them back was to attack the center, and suiting the action to the word, Attucks led the attack, and was the first to fall. Three whites were also killed, and the four heroes were buried in the same grave within a short distance of where Faneuil Hall now stands. Their memory is embalmed in the following lines:

"Long as in freedom's cause the wise contend,
Dear to your country shall your fame extend;
While to the world the lettered stone shall tell
Where Caldwell, Attucks, Gray and Manerick fell."

It was another Negro, Peter Salem, who advanced to the front of the line at the battle of Bunker Hill and killed Major Pitcairn, the British commander. Still another Negro, named Prince, captured General Prescott, the British commander, at Newport, Rhode Island. Lieutenant-Colonel Barton laid the plan for the capture of the British commander, and took with him the courageous Negro, Prince. Evading the guards, the two men, Col. Barton and his black attendant, reached the mansion in which slept the British general. It was necessary to force two strongly-locked doors, and these were burst open by Prince butting them open. Coming into the bedchamber of General Prescott, unattended by any other than Prince, Barton captured the British commander, which, in turn, led to his exchange for Gen. Lee, who had previously fallen into the hands of the British.

It is not generally known that many Negro troops fought in the ranks of the American army throughout the Revolution. Of one of these, Salem Poor, honorable mention is made by fifteen white men, in the American army, who memorialized Congress in his behalf, in the following language:

"To set forth the particulars of his conduct would be tedious; we only beg leave to say, in the person of this said Negro (Salem Poor) centers a brave, gallant soldier. The reward due so great and distinguished a character, we submit to Congress."

In the beginning of the Revolution it was understood that the Negroes who served as soldiers would be rewarded by their freedom at the close, but this was not done. Much more could be said of the Negro troops during the Revolution, but space forbids.* His conspicuousness in the Federal army dur-

*The following proclamation was issued by General Andrew Jackson a few months before the battle of New Orleans:
"Headquarters of 7th Military District.
"Mobile, September 21, 1814.
"To the free colored inhabitants of Louisiana:
"Through a mistaken policy you have heretofore been deprived of a participation in the glorious struggle for national rights in which our country is engaged. This no longer shall exist. As sons of freedom, you are called upon to defend our most inestimable blessing. As Americans, your country looks with confidence to her adopted children for a valorous support, as a faithful return for the advantages enjoyed under her mild and equitable government. As fathers, husbands and brothers, you are summoned to rally around the standard of the eagle, to defend all which is dear in existence.
"Your country, although calling for your exertions, does not wish you to engage in her cause without amply remunerating you for the services rendered. Your intelligent minds are not to be led away by false representations. Your love of honor would cause you to despise the man who would attempt to deceive you. In the sincerity of a soldier and the language of truth I address you. To every noble-hearted, generous freeman of color, volunteering to serve during the present contest with Great Britain, and no longer, there will be paid the same bounty in money and lands, now received by the white soldiers of the United States, viz.: one hundred and twenty-four dollars in money, and one hundred and sixty acres of land. The non-commissioned officers and privates will also be entitled to the same monthly pay and daily rations, and clothes, furnished to any American soldier.
"On enrolling yourselves in companies, the major-

ing the Civil War is well known, and it is also well known that measures were adopted to arm the Negro for the Confederate service near the close of the war, but its abrupt termination prevented the effort. Equally may it be said that the Negro was prominent in the war with Spain, but it is not so much about the martial history of the race that I would speak, as it is concerning his service in other spheres.

general commanding will select officers for your government from your white fellow-citizens. Your non-commissioned officers will be appointed from among yourselves. Due regard will be paid to the feelings of freemen and soldiers. You will not, by being associated with white men in the same corps, be exposed to improper comparisons or unjust sarcasm. As a distinct, independent battalion or regiment, pursuing the path of glory, you will undivided, receive the applause of gratitude of your countrymen.

"To assure you of the sincerity of my intentions, and my anxiety to engage your valuable services to our country, I have communicated my wishes to the Governor of Louisiana, who is fully informed as to the manner of enrollment, and will give you every necessary information on the subject of this address.

"Andrew Jackson,
"Major-General Commanding."

This is taken from Nile's Register, Vol. vii, p. 205.

From the same source on pages 345, 346 will be found the fact that Adjutant General Edward Livingston, read to the colored troops of Jackson's army, on December 18, 1814, the following address:

"To the men of color: Soldiers! From the shores of Mobile I collected you to arms. I invited you to share in the perils and to divide the glory of your white countrymen. I expected much from you, for I was not uninformed of those qualities which must render you formidable to an invading foe. I knew that you could endure hunger and thirst and all the hardships of war. I knew that you loved the land of your nativity, and that, like yourselves, you had to defend all that is most dear to man. But you surpass my hopes. I have found in you, united to these qualities, that noble enthusiasm which

The history of the Negro has been singularly marked by loyalty and devotion to the white race, which race enslaved him and made him a drudge and burden-bearer for centuries. As the great tides of influence and affluence swept on, the Negro was kept in a subjected condition, toiling and suffering, not only in an uncomplaining way, but in his innocence, singing as he went. His plantation melodies, quaint poetic nature, weird superstitions, and undiminished fealty are a part of our American history. His is a strange story, one of pathos, of romance, and of love to the white man, even in the depths of servitude. Of the wrangles in the press, on the platform, and in the nation's forum concerning himself, most of them knew but little, and many nothing at all. To him his past history was as blank as his destiny was dark. The great mass knew of nothing else than that they were to labor for the white man. The slave was subject to his beck and call, in season and out of season, never rebelling, never resisting, never revolting, but docilely toiling on.

Among the races of men the Negro has his domi-

impels to great deeds. Soldiers! The President of the United States shall be informed of your conduct on the present occasion; and the voice of the representatives of the American nation shall applaud your valor, as your general now praises your ardor. The enemy is near. His sails cover the lakes. But the brave are united; and if he finds us contending among ourselves it will be for the prize of valor and fame, its noblest reward."

This was also signed by General Jackson, and delivered in his name.

nant characteristic. That of the European or Anglo-Saxon is energy, and love of dominion; that of the American Indian, is revenge; that of the Malay, is craftiness; that of the Mongolian, is theft; that of the Negro, is docility, submissiveness. This quiet passive virtue has made him largely subordinate to others, hence his history of long enslavements. Of this disposition the most aggressive and progressive race has taken advantage, and for centuries held the black man in bondage.

To trace the history of African slavery through the territories and the states would require a separate and independent volume, and the matter will be given here only so much notice as is necessary to serve the present purpose. The idea of general emancipation was preceded by that of abolition of the slave trade. In 1787 a society for the suppression of the slave trade was formed in London. This led to the abolishment of the slave trade by Great Britain, which was followed by the United States and other portions of the world which had been engaged in the traffic. However, slavery continued as an institution, till its final overthrow in 1865. Some of the states had previously abolished slavery outright, and others by means of gradual emancipation. Positive action was taken by Vermont in 1777; by Massachusetts, in 1780; New York began the gradual emancipation process in 1799, and finally abolished slavery in 1827; New Jersey began the same plan in 1804, and had 236 slaves still living as late

as 1850, and Pennsylvania began gradual emanei-
pation in 1780, and by 1840 had 64 slaves within its
territory.

The favorable conditions of climate and of fertile
soil in the newer states of the South, made that region the last rendezvous of the American slave.
The slave traffic continued in the South till the beginning of hostilities between the states in 1861.
On the broad and rich cotton fields of the South the
slave was exceedingly remunerative, and the valuation of slave property led to the encouragement of
the increase of the race. The production of the
dominant staple, cotton, in increasing quantities,
under slave labor, year by year, led to the prosperity
of the two sections, notably of the states of the
South, and of those of New England. Even while
New England was the storm center of abolitionism
its cotton mills were steadily maintained by the staple produced by the Southern slave.

The agitation of the question of the freedom of
the slave once begun, it was continued with increasing force and fervor, till in consequence of the discussion of that and of cognate questions, the states
were plunged into war. The intensity of opposition to slavery was answered by equal intensity by
those who advocated the perpetuity of the institution. Views were resolved into what were regarded
as settled principles, and the utterances of certain
leaders fell but little short of the oracular in the
estimation of the masses. An illustration of this

principle was afforded in a famous deliverance from Hon. Alexander H. Stephens on the occasion of what is called his famous "Corner-Stone speech," at Savannah, Georgia, in the early days of 1861, and just a short while before the fall of Ft. Sumter. Among other things, he said: "Many governments have been founded upon the principle of subordination and serfdom of certain classes of the same race. Such were, and are, in violation of the laws of nature. Our system contains no such violation of nature's laws. With us, all the white race, however high or low, rich or poor, are equal in the eye of the law. Not so with the Negro; subordination is his place." Then referring to the new-born Confederacy, he further said: "Its foundations are laid, its corner-stone rests upon the great truth that the Negro is not equal to the white man, that slavery, subordination to the superior race, is his natural and normal condition!" Still further on, in the same address, Mr. Stephens gives emphasis to that already quoted, by saying: "It is upon this, as I have stated, our social fabric is firmly planted, and I cannot permit myself to doubt the ultimate success of the full recognition of this principle throughout the civilized and enlightened world." It was utterances like these which made the conditions of slavery ideal in the estimation of the great mass of the Southern people.

Not to trace further the history of slavery in the states, we turn now to a brief review of

the industrial and commercial worth of the Negro
to America. When the nineteenth century opened
the region extending from the Chattahoochee
westward to the Pacific was one of primeval forests and rolling prairies, scarcely touched by the
hand of art, save here and there in Louisiana and
Texas, there were settlements of foreign folk, the
improvements of whom were the scantiest, and their
efforts at development the feeblest. The useless
magnificence of Nature slumbered in the rich soil,
unwarmed by the sun, because of the dense foliage;
the rivers rolled wanton to the sea, and the price-
less ores slumbered untouched by the pick. Herculean strength was needed to level the forests, to
drain and fence the land, and to evoke the slumber-
ing wealth from the alluvial soil. Semitropical heat
and the poison of malaria had to be encountered by
a fortified muscularity which the Anglo-Saxon had
not, but which the African had. Consequently the
African was summoned to the gigantic task.

A half century later the forests had disappeared,
and expansive plantations of corn, cotton, cane, and
other products overspread the same vast region, dot-
ted here and there with emporiums and marts of
trade, the bustle and din of which filled the land;
steamboats plied the broad rivers laden with their
cargoes of value, and railways ramified in every
direction as arteries of commerce; ships came and
went from the ports, giving and receiving argosies
of wealth; colleges throve where once savage life

reigned supreme, and homes sumptuous and luxurious adorned with domestic tranquillity the wide expanse throughout. This mighty transformation was wrought by the labor of the slave. While generations of whites with increasing affluence passed to their tombs, living in the luxury produced by the slave, while living, and dying, their last resting places were marked by stately column and mausoleum, themselves the product of slave labor, the slave himself, toiling beneath the heat, with just a sufficiency of coarse food to give him vitality to labor, passed in a procession of generations to humble graves, unmarked by art, and soon leveled to the surface, and covered by tangled vines and riotous weeds. Through his lucrative labor, luxury, wealth, education, and refinement were produced to the enrichment of the nation, while the share of the slave was ignorance, vice, penury, servitude, an humble cabin, and a few feet of earth where he found at last a resting place for his worn and aged body.

Not the South alone was developed in its wealth, but New England and the Middle States as well, and, for that matter, indirectly old England also, for the cotton of the South became one of the chief products of the wealth of the world. With the monumental wealth thus built and cemented by the sweat of the Negro slave, can it now be said that the Negro has forfeited all claim to the consideration of the American whites, because of his blunders and misdeeds? With the history of an enriched continent behind it, and with the ashes of seven generations sleeping in the soil of America, is there nothing in a history so tragic to appeal to a stronger race to inspire this same race of blacks to higher planes of life?

The question is not one of mere sentiment, it is one of profound principle. Here are the monuments of the slave's labor; here are the products of his toil in the prosperity which is today enjoyed. Can we disregard our obligation to this race of ex-slaves, and dismiss the matter with a sneer? To the Christian religion, by its injection into the world, is the bondman indebted for the elimination of slavery. When Christianity appeared, slavery was inextricably involved in the society of the world, and it seemed as firmly rooted in human society as are the Apennines in the substance of *I*taly. Entering on the mission of reforming society from within outward, abuses fled, and arrogance fell before its sway. As fast as its power widened over the world, slavery grew gradually milder, weaker, less crushing, narrower in its range, and more merciful in its rule, until it ceased altogether.

But the work of Christianity is not yet done with respect to the lately enslaved race in these American states. The school is most .valuable, and it should be made more expansive and thorough in its work as an invaluable adjunct to Christian effort. Despite the efforts and clatter of the cheap politician and the mountebank author and lecturer, in opposition to the Negro, the spirit of education is abroad in the land, but the higher and sterner assertion of the ethics of the gospel must be felt more potently, if we would dissolve the grave difficulty of the prodigious race problem. American Christianity must face the issue and by an insertion of its principles into other agencies, into all agencies indeed, the fulcrum of the gospel must be brought into play to elevate a race which is present by the coercion of our forefathers, a race which has laid the foundation of our national wealth, thereby imposing on the present generation of whites a double obligation. Who will dare say that the gospel in its application to this great question will prove inefficacious? Sheer gratitude on the part of the American Christian should incite to aidful action in behalf of the Negro. A lofty sense of duty, independent of gratitude, should impel to his assistance, and the claims of the Negro to Christian agency are undeniable.

Let it be said again, that if the race was still in the throes of a degraded condition we could not spurn its claims, but since it is struggling, and by every possible sacrifice is seeking to raise itself to usefulness and respectability, the better among them seeking by every possible means to lift the fallen, is there not in view of these conditions an appeal pathetic and tragic which is made to the heart of every Christian? After the utmost that can be offered against the Negro be urged, Christian obligation remains. No amount of argumentation relieves the obligation; no evasion displaces it. The Negro is here, and in the providence of God he is destined to remain. He is a fixed element of our civilization. He is here by compulsion; he will remain here from necessity. As the recipients of his unrequited toil of centuries, shall we now show him only indifference and suffer him to scramble for a footing in the race for life? *Is* it the duty of the Christian public to regard with icy indifference the wrongs frequently done the Negro without a word of protest, and without the exercise of some effort in his behalf? To pursue a course other than that of substantial and helpful consideration, is at variance with the simplest principles of the gospel.

We have spoken of his contributions to the civilization of America; it has been shown how by his energy and sweat and life he has aided in building the nation; how he has transformed the wilderness into gardens of plenty and of beauty; how he has supplied the means of our splendid commerce and sent it over the world; how he has educated generations of our people while his share has been that of dismal ignorance; how he has fed our armies, shielded our families, guarded our interests with a jealousy that was remarkable and without parallel in the history of peoples; how, when liberated, he took up his line of march, he knew not whither, without means, without knowledge, without experience, and yet emerging from a condition like this, he has made himself worthy by his own merit; how he is struggling against the odds still frowning before him and disputing his commendable efforts; how he does not pine and seek pity at the hands of a stronger race, but with herculean struggle is seeking to overcome—is there not in all this a pathetic appeal to the heart of Christianity? Nor has the Negro ceased to be useful and a producer of prosperity. His accumulated millions of property are a material fact patent alike to all. As he advances and is elevated, his usefulness expands, his devotion to country increases, his value as a resident and citizen improves, his power of production of wealth is enhanced.

Does this condition not impose an additional obligation on the Caucasian Christian of America to extend to the "brother in black" every possible means of protection and of assistance?. Let each answer for himself.

CHAPTER VII.

SERIOUS BARRIERS TO NEGRO PROGRESS.

Few stop sufficiently long to consider the immense disadvantages with which the Negro is compelled to battle in order to gain a footing as a man and citizen, in demonstration of his right to live, and be respected on the scene of his late servitude. Like the bird emerging from its shell into the wide universe of being, without moving the distance of an inch, the Negro has been delivered from his bonds and the narrow confines of his servitude without stirring beyond his original habitat, and ushered into a universe of limitless possibility. It has been a change of condition and of relation rather than one of linear measurement. Right within sight of the old plantation and the remembered scenes of its exacting discipline, the cabin of discomfort and the graveyard hardby—right in the midst of scenes like these must the mettle of the race be tested, its virtues tried.

How poorly equipped the Negro was for the initial encounters with the surrounding difficulties, we each know. With what he had to contend by contact with the best qualified race of the globe, we know, and the disadvantage with which he had to begin the struggle, we are each aware. Nominally free, he was handicapped by ignorance, inexperience, and by the absence of means with which even to make a beginning. This was the first serious barrier encountered by the race to which freedom suddenly came, and every one recognizes that difficulties such as have been named would have been serious to any people. In daily contact with his original owner, with relations between them now radically changed, with the former master smarting under the sting and humiliation of defeat, and the deeper and sorer sting of a wrecked fortune, a large part of which the Negro himself was, was itself not an indifferent factor in the sum of disadvantages with which the ex-slave had to contend. Whether thought of or not, these barriers were of a most serious character to the recently enslaved man in black. Add to this the more serious and distressing condition of poverty bequeathed to the Negro in his emancipation. Absolutely penniless, four and a half million people were turned adrift on the world with no hope but that which would come of the exercise of sheer muscle. The world never before witnessed a condition like this with respect to any people.

Great as these disadvantages were, they were trifling compared with those which were destined to follow. Sadly duped into the corruptest of political conditions, conditions which will require many years to overcome, and made the victim and the scapegoat of a system concocted by the worst of men, who preyed on the credulity of the ignorant Negro to his own fell disadvantage, the wonder is that the race was able at all to survive the ordeal. Here was the most serious crisis of the Negro, and one that met him at the threshold of his new-born freedom. Had the Negro gone to work deliberately to engender an aversion, the deepest of which the whites were capable, he could not have more effectually succeeded. Yet in all this the Negro was not so blameworthy as were the vultures who fattened on his mistakes, and when the worst had been done, these same harpies fled, leaving the Negro to shoulder the consequences. Here as elsewhere the Negro in his relations to others was at a grave disadvantage. Could the scenes and events crowded into the tragical drama of reconstruction been averted, the Iliad of the Negro's woes would never have been so great. In the light of the subsequent capabilities of the Negro, his original barriers might have been easily overcome; but with an incubus like this, all his other advantages were aggravated. The graver lent emphasis to the lesser.

But then his difficulties did not end here. He is a man with a dark skin which is the inevitable occasion of aversion to the white races. This has been true in all ages, and was the occasion of the serious rupture between the great lawgiver, Moses, and his brother and sister, because the renowned brother had taken for a wife the Cushite woman.*

Besides all this, still, the Southern Negro had been a slave, and this stigma he has to bear, no matter what his merits be. This, too, has always been an obstruction to an enslaved race, till it has been able to be overcome by time. To the Negro it is a peculiar disadvantage in the South for reasons that are obvious. In spite of himself, and in spite of his promptings of generosity, the Anglo-Saxon is arrogant in his assertion among other races which he may touch.

Wherever found over the globe, he is self-assertive and dominating in spirit. This is not said captiously, but stated as a mere fact. He must be superior or nothing. That superiority is claimed by himself wherever he has found his place on the globe. Brought into contact with the proudest segment of the Anglo-Saxon race, the ex-slave, a black man, was at once at a disadvantage. Any one of the disadvantages named would have been serious in the pathway of a race similarly conditioned, but all of them were the Negro's. How has the Negro met these difficulties? The answer is found in his achievements during the last thirty years, for his exploits as a race did not begin till after the throes of years. It is answered by a leadership which chal-

*See Numbers XII, and especially Geike's "Old Testament Characters," p. 122, and Birch's "Ancient Egypt," p. 81.

lenges the admiration of all; by the 32,000 youths
of the Negro race engaged in the acquirement of
trades and valuable occupations; in the 300,000
farms purchased and owned by the Negroes; by the
400,000 homes built and owned by the race; by the
fifty or more banks established and maintained by
Negro capital; by the 10,000 places of business
found in the cities of the country; by the $600,000,-
000 worth of taxable property in the possession of
Negro owners; by the 28,000 public schools manned
by 30,000 Negro teachers; by the 170 industrial
schools and colleges conducted by the Negroes of
the country, and by the 23,000 ministers, and
26,000 churches owned and paid for by the Negroes, to say nothing of the large number of missionaries on the distant and different fields of the
globe.

Facing the future with a will and a pluck undaunted by difficulty, and led by men of wisdom and
of expansive policies and of great achievement, the
Negro has made himself an exception among the
peoples of the earth in the rapidity of his advancement. Never was a more herculean task undertaken, than was that of the Negro in his emergence
from the environment by which he was at first beset
behind and before, and never were achievements
more signal. Here are the facts to speak for themselves. We may answer some things, but facts we
must accept. The penalty of leadership was never
greater than was that imposed on the intrepid **men**

and women who essayed to lead their people out of
the tangled wilderness of difficulty in which they
found themselves a few years after the boon of
emancipation came. What was the task imposed
on these daring and untutored leaders, few in number, and themselves forced to pick slight advantages
along the way—the task coolly assumed, with difficulties blocking every inch of the struggling march?
Though themselves once young slaves, and bearing
the traditional reproach of such consequences, they
placed themselves beneath the burden of lifting to
a higher place in life millions of ignorant, black and
despised ex-slaves. More than that, these same
leaders had largely to assume the responsibility of
the numerous shortcomings of as stolid a mass of
ignorance as ever sought to follow. As the years
have gone, there have been rained on the devoted
heads of these pioneers of the race abuse and male-
diction not a little, but with philosophic serenity
they have met it all, and are still doing so. In their
bewildering struggles these primary leaders were
beset behind and before—behind by a tremendous
load which they were seeking to draw; before, by
barriers which required the utmost tact and skill to
overcome. How well the task has been performed,
let the monuments of their labors tell. These daunt-
less spirits of a despised race will go down in history
as the builders of a new race, unencumbered by the
traditions of a past. To them the unwritten and
unlettered history of a Dark Continent is an abso-

lute blank. This is what has been aptly called the re-emergence of Africa in another and distant land. They have set in operation agencies which are full of prophetic meaning. They have astonished the age with their tremendous strides. They have silenced opposition, once rife and popular, that the race would rapidly decay and pass away. They have hushed into muteness the clamor once raised that in individual endeavor they would fail, and lapse again into barbarism. They have adjusted themselves to the favoring breezes of the times, and are being borne toward the same port of destiny as are others. *In* scholastic work, in industry, in commerce, in manufacture, in the creation of wealth, in missionary endeavor in distant parts, in all that enters into modern life, they are quietly coming and bringing to pass. And all this is being accomplished in spite of the difficulties strong and formidable met at every step of the way. They have but little without to cheer, much to retard. They have been scorned, ridiculed, obstructed, and yet the march has been an onward one. They have illustrated the spirit of the lines of Gerald Massey:

> "We are beaten back in many a fray,
>   But newer strength we borrow;
> Where the vanguard rests today,
>   The rear shall camp tomorrow."

With an optimism peculiar to the race, they have declined to be hindered by the past and move with unquailing front toward the future. While others have philosophized about their incompetency and prophesied their racial doom, they have quietly toiled like the coral insect in the depths, building their fortunes, and rooting deep their own cherished institutions.

If under the burden of the difficulties already recounted, ignorance, inexperience, poverty, the imposition of vicious white men prompted by fell design, the paralysis of the drinking den, racial opposition and obstruction, and the bitter residuum of it all, which was the sum total left the Negro—if from conditions like these he could rally and climb so far up the hill within so brief a span of years, he should now be able, with advantages immensely superior, to intensify the brightness of his future. When the jubilee of their emancipation shall come, the Negroes of America should be able, in some substantial and spectacular way, to demonstrate by an accumulation of illustrations of their achievements these facts in some central exposition. The history of their successes is known only in part; let it be grouped in tangible shape and set before the eyes of the world. By an exposition of this kind prejudicial barriers will largely give place to encouraging wonder and surprise, and fresh inspiration will be imparted to many lagging spirits of the race.

One of the essential necessities of the Negro race just now is, an exalted racial pride. One who is ashamed of being a Negro and who assumes to ape others is unworthy of the race. It should be the aspiration of every negro to invest the name of the race with honor, dignity, and worth. With a racial patriotism like this, a patriotism which inspires other races, an increasing propulsion will be given the upward movement of the Negro people. Standing full in the gaze of the world for almost a half century, as its fortunes have ebbed and flowed in a mighty grapple with impediments of every kind, and wringing victory from multiplied catastrophes and calamities, the Negro has awakened questions as to the limit of the possibility of accomplishment of his race, as well as the possible effect of his people on the future destiny of the country and of the world. That which was once exceptional in the leadership of the race, which itself was discounted because it was esteemed as only exceptional, and therefore proving nothing for the Negro race as a whole, is annually becoming more common, as the ranks of the worthy are swelling and their accomplishments are multiplying.

Yet while much has been done, much more remains to be done. There are still numerous obstructions to be met, many difficulties to be overcome. From present indications there is no primrose path for the Negro in the years of the immediate future. On his merit he must rely in the future as in the past. He must insist on making himself an indispensable adjunct of American civilization. In all the stations occupied, from the lowliest boot-black on the streets to the office of the bank president and the professor's chair in the institution of learning, his proficiency must be such as to make him an object of demand. This has been the spirit of such schools as those at Hampton and Tuskegee, and of others as well; this has animated the business interests established and maintained throughout the country, and this principle must be sternly maintained. Confidence is the pivot of the Negro's ultimate hope of success. Because of the traditional defects attributed to the race in the past, the eye of the public will be more keenly riveted on this than on any other element which will enter into the life and success of the Negro. That this confidence is steadily growing in public esteem, and growing because of that which the Negro has accomplished, is evident on all hands. He must discourage lawlessness, must inspire virtue, must awaken yet more and more integrity. In cool disregard of obstructions in the past he has pressed on, and has, in innumerable instances, pushed his way to success. To abate this spirit one jot or tittle, would mean his downward turn in life. To compel the public recognition of merit by wisely-directed pluck and unabated persistency is the fulcrum by means of which the race will steadily rise in the American states. That these have been many times illustrated in the achievements wrought by Negroes, is an earnest of the future success of the race.

Booker Washington beginning at Tuskegee in a chicken-house for a school-room, and a blind mule and one hoe on a few acres of land, and that poor; beginning at a time when prejudice against the Negro was supreme, and evolving from contemptible conditions like these the greatest Negro industrial institution in the world, with its more than a hundred buildings of architectural attractiveness, all built by materials manufactured by the students themselves and erected by these same students; with the halls yearly thronged by from fourteen to fifteen hundred students; Boyd assuming to establish a publishing plant at Nashville, without a cent of capital, and yet succeeding in the erection of a plant within a few years the value of which is quoted by Dun at $313,000; Pettiford opening a savings bank in the city of Birmingham by placing a table for the receipt of deposits, and after a few years having a capital stock of more than $40,000, with authorized stock of $100,000, and with deposits of $132,000; Groves working at forty cents a day on a potato farm in Kansas, and now worth $100,000, and the acknowledged "potato king" of Kansas; Preston Taylor, the preacher-financier of Nashville, an original slave lad from Louisiana, now worth $250,000; R. F. Boyd, a country lad reared on a farm in Giles County, Tennessee, now one of the most skillful surgeons in Nashville, irrespective of color, and a man who has amassed a fortune; Harry Todd, of Darien, Georgia, once a slave, but now worth $600,-000, the wealthiest Negro in Georgia, and hundreds of others, that might be named, are the illustrations of what the Negro is accomplishing.

Yet a little more than a generation ago, some of these whose names and successes are here recorded, were slaves in the cramped quarters on Southern plantations. Each has met every adverse condition raised in his way, has conquered it, and become an accomplished success.

It is not an exaggeration to say that some others of the races would have gone to pieces under the collisions, catastrophes, and disasters of various kinds encountered by the Negroes, but by dint of flexible pluck, thousands of them have attained to eminence in agricultural, commercial, scholastic, and professional life, and are worthy of the highest meed of praise.

CHAPTER VIII.

VALUE OF THE NEGRO TO OUR CIVILIZATION.

The well-nigh all-pervasive idea of commercialism in the American mind reduces almost every question to the basis of the single principle—"Will it pay?" The estimate of causes and movements, of whatever kind, turns largely on this question, and the consequent decision of acceptance or rejection is founded, for the most part, on this idea.

It is proposed to discuss the so-called Negro question from this commercial point of view, or to raise and face the question fairly and frankly as to whether, after all, it is worth while to shield and protect the Negro against imposition, and to seek to promote his welfare, or whether we shall crush him as an unworthy element of civilization. Wherein lies the intrinsic advantage of protecting, defending, and promoting the welfare of the Negro? In the prosecution of a policy like this, would there accrue any value to the community or to the country at large? After all, is the Negro worth it? Is there a probability that there would be any financial return commensurate with the expenditure of interest in his behalf? Is the presence of the Negro one of value or of disadvantage, especially to the states of the South?

Aside from all other considerations such as those of humanity, philanthropy, or Christianity, which are elsewhere discussed in the present volume, let us see if there is a financial remuneration connected with his continued presence among us. Considering now alone, as far as possible, our relation to the subject in its bald financial aspect, would there be a correspondingly remunerative return, if the Negro were granted conditions by means of which he could enjoy an unbroken sense of protection by the guarantee of simple justice which is constitutionally provided for all alike, and which finds expression in the democratic axiom—"Equal rights to all, special privileges to none?"

It is a principle of common observation relative to all classes of our people, and certainly of the industrial history of the Negro race during the last few decades, that so soon as security is given, improvement begins. Assure every man of the fruits of his exertions, and of his certain protection equally with all, and a fresh spirit is excited for worthy accomplishment, and he is naturally incited to his best endeavor. Everywhere the principle obtains that security produces industry, while insecurity equally produces idleness and criminality. Men can be induced to work by only two motives—hope and fear; the former the motive of the free laborer, the latter, that of the slave.

It is but the statement of a fact commonly known, that there is a large minority of the sentiment of the white population of the people of the South which is opposed to the Negro. Without now stopping to name the alleged grounds of such opposition, it can be said as a matter of fact, that some of this opposition shows itself in forms that are moderate, extending no further than to expressions of contempt, scorn or ridicule, while much of it is quite hostile, manifesting itself in different forms of imposition, and sometimes in acts of cruelty and in shocking expressions of violence. Not infrequently from this hostile class come such expressions as, "*I*t were better if we had no Negroes in the country." It is fair to assume that this and similar expressions are the result of hasty and inconsiderate speech, rather than of serious sentiment. There are not wanting among such, and they, of course, the more reasonable, those who when the subject is reduced to logical demonstration, will materially modify such sentiments.

In order that the question may be brought fully before us on its merits, and the flimsiness of a position like this be shown, let us suppose it possible to remove, in a single day, every Negro from the country. Let every place occupied by him in the home, as a cook, hostler, gardener, butler, porter, or waiter; every farm, mine, shop, school—every place be vacated by the Negro, how many of those who now reproach him would consent to this? A partial illustration of the howl of objection which would be raised to a procedure like this is afforded now and then, when agents from one part of the South invade other parts to offer peculiar inducements to laborers to remove elsewhere. On occasions like this, it has sometimes been interesting to note what a popular uprising is produced against the removal of the much-hated Negro.

But to all this it may be said in reply that the Negro is the only source of labor, but if he were out of the way, other laborers would supply his place. What others? This question brings us to the core of the discussion. No one at all familiar with labor conditions in this and in other countries, can be unaware of the fact that in a number of respects, so far as the South is concerned, the labor of the Negro surpasses that of any other. Nor can the proposition be questioned by any one of fair and candid mind, that the capabilities of the Negro, as a class, expand and develop in proportion to his opportunities to improve.

If again the answer be made that white men till the lands in other parts of the country, and can do so here, if necessity demands, it is only sufficient to say, in reply, that white laborers in the West and Northwest would be unable to perform the same amount of labor beneath the burning suns of the South. Yet, if it still be said that white men by the thousand labor on the fields of the South, it must be borne in mind that their tillage is, almost without exception, confined to the lighter and thinner soils.

Who sees white men tilling the stiff, heavy and fertile soils of the Southern states—soils the staple product of which has made the South famous throughout the world? The large planters of the South, in recognition of the fact that the power of endurance can be undergone by none so well as by the black laborer, rarely engage the services of a white man. Appreciating the value of the Negro laborer, these employers come by an instinctive law to prize the Negro as a man, and if they know his faults, they know his merits as well, and as a rule, this class is the readiest to defend him. Promiscuous and wholesale denunciation of the Negro rarely comes from this class of Southern whites. If they pity, and sympathize with the weaker elements among them, they equally applaud the worth and merit of the others. Never from this class of whites come abuse and violence. No one ever hears from this representative class of Southerners an apprehension of that delusive fad and politically popular will-o'-the-wisp — social equality. Representative people like these have no fear that their social standing is in danger of being impaired by the Negro. It is altogether from another class that the apprehension of social equality comes. The power of endurance and the muscularity of the Negro, his ability and promptness to meet the many-sided demands made on him, his proverbial tractableness and responsiveness have served him as a bulwark of defense, while conjoined with this has been the rein-

forcement of many white friends who know his
worth, and in numerous instances have intervened
to shield him from violence. The fact that the
Negro holds his place against the peoples of the
world, as the laborer preferred above all others on
the lands of the South, establishes his worth beyond
question. The Negro population is a vast mine of
wealth which needs only development and encouragement to make it profitable beyond calculation.

Up to this time we have considered the Negro
only as a subordinate, as a subsumed manual laborer.
Now let us go a step further and consider him as
an independent producer of wealth in the direction
and management of his own affairs. His ability
to accumulate so much wealth under so many dispir-
iting conditions, within the short period of only
forty-five years, illustrates the capability of the
Negro, and his intrinsic worth to the country. If
the taxable property alone of the Negro population
was divided equally among the members of the race,
each would have per capita fully sixty dollars. This
would include every infant, every indigent old man
and woman, every criminal. In other words, the
aggregate valuation of the taxable property of the
race amounts to about $600,000,000, all of which
has been acquired within less than fifty years, and
that under contrary conditions, and in the first stage
of the freedom of that people. Give the Negro
forty-five years more with his increasing knowledge,
his aptness to acquire, aspiration to improve and

advance, expanding power, and developing skill, remarkable readiness to adjust himself to conditions, and who can foresee what his contributions to the wealth of the nation will be within the next half century?

Above many things, Americans want producers of capital. There is scarcely an American town or community which would not warmly welcome any man who is a producer of wealth. The wealth of no one is of any value unless it is distributed in the community according to the laws which control money as a circulating medium. The more wealth one creates, the more does he bestow on the community, according to the general principles of trade. *I*t may be the result of brawn or brain, or of both— it is created and therefore dispensed. If a population as unpromising as the ex-slaves of the South were, in the outset, can accomplish so much in the very teeth of fierce competition, what may these people not yield to the country, if protected and given justice and security in the full exercise of unhampered powers?

As a laborer, the Negro is the cheapest; as a citizen, he is the most frugal; as a business man, he is economical; as an American, he spends his money at home, and does not transmit it to another and remote region, as do many others who have sought residence in the Union. Maltreated by advantage taken of him by designing men, does he sulk and repine? Is he revengeful and threatening? Every

fair man knows that these things are not true of
him.

But the story of the Negro's worth is yet but im-
perfectly told. To show the utter hollowness of
much of the inconsiderate and flippant denunciation
of the Negro, largely because it is a fashion thus to
indulge in cheap twaddle, it is known as a well
established fact, that many who give vent to sentiments like these, do so often while in the enjoyment
of the services of colored domestics or employes.
There is the unconscious satisfaction of having such
service, while there is, at the same time, the disposition to indulge in abuse. An apt illustration of this
was met with in a Southern home, where there were
several children who were entrusted to the care of
a Negro nurse, rather an elderly woman, though
alert and active. Her control of this group in the
sitting room and at the dining table, seemed to be
absolute, even though the parents were present.
This is by no means an uncommon condition in a
Southern home. It was observed that her management and discipline was perfect, as was shown by
an occasional "Ah!" attended by the pointing of the
index finger of the old woman, in response to which
the urchin would stop short his utterance or unseemly conduct. At one time, when the servant
disappeared for a short while, the father found no
stronger motive of appeal to one of the little boys
than to say, "Better mind, Mammy will get you!"
For nine-tenths of the time these children were

under the control of that careful nurse. When at
last the old woman disappeared with her group of
dependents, the father remarked to the interested
guest that the old servant had been with them for
a number of years, and that she was regarded as an
indispensable adjunct of that home, and that he
could not see how her services could be dispensed
with. The care, the character, and largely the destiny of those children were lodged in the hands of
that old black mammy. Yet when the conversation
turned on a casual discussion of the Negro question,
the language seemed inadequate to furnish terms
sufficiently harsh to enable him to express his antipathy to the race. His abuse was so indiscrimi-
nately wholesale that one would have thought the
race of Negroes, without exception, was to him a
favorite aversion. The writer happened to know
that neither he nor his immediate ancestors were
ever the owners of slaves. This illustrates the
phase of spoken expression without a practical
source of sentiment so prevalent in many quarters
of the South.

But to proceed further. Notwithstanding the
common abuse to which the Negro is subjected
partly from habit, as has been shown, and partly
because of racial hostility, the fact remains that he
has all along been the guardian of protection to
Southern society. He is usually considered and
spoken of as a standing menace to the interests of
society, and as endangering, by his presence, the

safety of our institutions; yet the fact that he has been our chief cordon of defense needs only to be stated to be recognized.

Suppose the millions of blacks had not been in the South during several decades past, occupying the multitudinous stations of usefulness which they hold, whom should we have in their stead? Millions of the scum of southern Europe or of the Orient. With inherited vice, moral obliquity, criminality, infidelity, socialistic and anarchical ideas, we should have had them by the million in the homes, the places of business, and on the farms of the South. Bad as so many claim, often without reason, our condition to be, it would be immeasurably worse but for the presence of the Negro. Having him, what have we? A docile, tractable, unrevengeful race, a people whom we know, and have known for centuries; a race which has demonstrated its loyalty to the white race in innumerable ways; that is anxious to remain among us, and from abused conditions raises only now and then a subdued protest, and oftener than otherwise appeals to the stronger race; which in the weakness of its numbers as compared with those of the stronger race, implores protection from the commercial aggrandizement, official imposition and abuse, and judicial injustice, from which it suffers; a people ambitious to advance to wider spheres of usefulness and respectability; a race without infidels, without the mafia or black-hand organizations, without disloyalty to the flag of our common country, without a deeply-nourished grudge, and in full accord with the genius of our institutions.

Place the one element of population over against the other, and what choice would even the most hostile enemy of the Negro race make? The presence of the faithful Negro has kept back the inroads of a most undesirable population which would have brought a train of evils and vices, debauchery and demoralization, and crimes nameless and without number. A servant population we should have had, and if not Negro, what other? None other would have been available than that already named.

Then, is the Negro of any value? Has he ever been of use and worth? Are not the possibilities abundant for making him more valuable still? The promotion of his interest as an industrial asset is the promotion of that of the community and state. With only partial encouragement he builds his places of business, establishes his banks, and insurance organizations, the progressive ones act as a constant stimulus to the others in the lower ranks, animating to thrift and habits of industry; he writes his books, not to excite passion and incendiarism but to create respectability—publishes his newspapers, only to incite to self-respect and racial advancement, while those on the higher rounds are constant in their endeavor to raise to loftier planes others struggling up from beneath. The Negro purchases land and tills it with profit to the commonwealth, establishes his home, his school, his church, and with each recurring year vindicates his claim to recognition because of his solid worth in contributing to the wealth of the community and the state. Is there nothing in the face of the facts, which are matters of every day observation even to the most casual observer, to appeal to the stronger and more favored race, if not for the sake of humanity, if not in the name of philanthropy, if not in the cause of Christianity, but purely because of his financial value—is there not sufficient in all this to call for a revision of much prevailing misconception and a reversal of so much ill-nature against the Negro? Is there not enough to appeal to every thoughtful man and woman among us to lend to the black man friendly help and support in his faithful endeavors?

In the preceding part of this chapter attention was called to certain facts, which are such as address themselves to us every day.

"To all facts there are laws,
The effect has its cause, and I mount to the cause."

Some things may be answered—facts cannot. The principles presented appeal to cool reason, not to passion. Now in spite of all these things there is a peculiar prejudicial disposition, sometimes even among the more thoughtful, to disparage and discount the worthiest efforts of the Negro. Beginning in the dawn of the Negro's freedom, some of the animadversions on the Negro have become traditional. The prediction was current and copious in the outset of his liberty, that when the supporting arm of the white man was withdrawn, and the Negro was left unpropped, he would return to his original paganism. However, the Negro preferred the opposite course. Slowly but with certainty, he began the ascent to a better and thriftier life. A leadership of worth emerged from his ranks, and by its wisdom and guidance astonished the world. What then? The prophecy failing, the predicters insisted that these were only sporadic exceptions such as we might find even among quadrupeds giving abnormal and unusual expressions of superiority. But instances of actual worth continued to multiply, and the prominent became more prominent still. The exception was fast resolving itself into the rule. Not the fulfilled prophecy, but the opposite had come to pass.

Then what? An accommodated twist was given to the protest at first raised against the Negro. Declining to return to the darkness of paganism, and preferring rather to grope his way to the light of the advantages afforded by civilized life in the midst of which he had been reared, and of which he was previously only a spectator, he brought himself conspicuously into the gaze of the world. The next stage of disparagement to which the unfriendly betook themselves was the institution of the comparative merits between the intellectual caliber of the two races. This was an unconscious compliment to the Negro, of whom it had been predicted only a few years before that he would lapse into the darkness of his jungle ancestry. Nor did the comparison stop there. The Negro was disparaged because he did not attain unto the standard of life and of progress which had been reached by his Anglo-Saxon neighbor. Because he had not at a single bound leaped the distance made by the whites after centuries of struggle and progress, he must be made a man of small worth. But there is an immense difference between a few decades, and many centuries.

To this the answer is sometimes made that the black man had only to enter on the inheritance of the civilization built by the white race. But this is a clear evasion of the issue. The question of advantage is not the point at issue, but that of the capability of the Negro race to grasp and appropriate civilized advantages, no matter whence they came. It is as equally true that the present generation of whites inherit the advantages of all the past, as that any other people does. The question is, Is the Negro capable of applying the privileges of our civilization in such a way as to be a promoter of prosperity, and if so, is he not worthy of at least an opportunity to demonstrate his full worth by the removal of the difficulties which dispute his progress and hinder his development?

We have seen how far short certain predictions concerning the Negro have fallen. We have observed his astonishing ascent to a station in civilization of which he was not at first thought to be capable. Since he has accomplished so much in so incredibly short time, it is a question what the Negro may be able to do in the years of the immediate future.

It must be borne in mind that all the dazzling accomplishments of the white race of modern times have been achieved within the last century. For eighteen hundred years the results of Anglo-Saxon civilization were comparatively primitive and bungling. All the centuries preceding that of the nineteenth were those of preparation, accumulation, formation, and assimilation.

As late as 1809 no steam propeller had ever plowed the waters of the globe; victories on battle fields had been won by flintlock muskets; in Great Britain, at that time, it cost fourteen pence, an equivalent of twenty-eight cents, to send a letter three hundred miles, and in the United States seventeen cents for the same service; there was not then a single iron-barred tramway on the globe, nor was there a known plow with iron or steel mold board; then the harvesters in every land of the world cut their grain with the primitive sickle; the most rapid transit on earth or sea was the sailing vessel propelled by the winds; the industrial genius of man was shown only in local enterprises and in articles of curious handiwork; the packhorse and clumsy stage-coach did the work of transportation on land; the science of geology was then unknown, and human knowledge of the solar system was limited to the orbit of Uranus; but little was known of the constitution of the earth and of the atmosphere which envelopes our globe; the greatest telescope in existence was the twenty-foot reflector of Herschel, and both Great Britain and the United States at that period fostered and defended human slavery.

It is worthy of note that in the year 1809 there were born into the world a group of notable men who have mightily shaped the destiny of the Anglo-Saxon race—Oliver Wendell Holmes, Edgar Allan Poe, Felix Mendelssohn, Charles Robert Darwin, Alfred Tennyson, William Ewart Gladstone, and Abraham Lincoln. These men, and others like them, the product of the centuries which had gone before, grasping the advantages within reach, and following divergent lines, lifted the race till, with its improvements, it came within the reach of another generation, and that another, all of which has packed within the compass of a single century the mightiest achievements known to time.

During all these preceding ages the latent possibilities which have fruited into realities were undreamed of. But their consummation was due to unfettered thought, and nothing stood in the way save the grim barriers of Nature. What hidden possibilities may exist in a race such as that of the Afro-American, possibilities of quite a different order, it may be, from those enumerated, but still great, if unhindered in the exercise of opportunity, no one can foretell, any more than forty-five years ago the success of the race attained by this time could have been foretold. That which has been done by the Negro is frankly acknowledged to be astounding, especially when we recall the unfavorable conditions which have been suspended at every step over his head.

At any rate, the Negro being a man, we dare not seek to make less of him, and if we venture to do so, no matter under what pretext, we fly into the face of Providence. Since his foot first touched American soil, the Negro's yearning has been Godward. He has his faults, his vices, his crimes, and in these respects he shares with all other races; but he is the most religious of the races of men. So far from returning to the fetishism of his ancestors on the Dark Continent, his general disposition has been heavenward, and his loyalty to his religion has itself been a mighty asset to our prosperity. He may have his superstition, but it is of a harmless sort, and has not attained to that rank of horrid tragedies which has involved the murder of hundreds of innocent people against whom there was no charge laid, save that of a superstitious notion that they were witches!

We return to the original question, *Is the Negro of any value to our civilization?* What verdict shall we render in the face of the facts just presented? *If* he be of value, are we the people to decry and discourage the struggling race, born and reared on American soil and loyal to all to which the more favored race is loyal, and in full attune with the

advancement of the times, and faithful even in discouragement to the whites? Is it the spirit of chivalry, of wisdom, and of practical judgment thus to
do, seeing the immense value of the colored race to
our civilization? Must we countenance and support
divers attempts to ·undervalue and depreciate the
commendable feats of that lesser and unfortunate
race? If within the span of a few years that people
have accomplished so much, what immense value
will they not prove within the next half-century?
If in all departments of industry and thrift we aim
at improvement, why should we not animate a race
of ten million people, the strides of whom within
forty-five years have been phenomenal? Improvement of vegetable and fruit products is sought with,
commendable assiduity year by year. The sciences
are invoked to aid in the propagation of improved
species alike in the vegetable and animal kingdoms,
and in the production of immaterial agencies to
benefit humanity. Lives of men and of women, too,
are being devoted with a beautiful consecration to
the development of various species of flower, fruit,
and four-footed beasts. Why not devote some such
attention to the elevation of a race which in spite
of verbal denial to the contrary, insists on producing
concrete illustrations of its mighty capabilities for
good? Why not at least clear the way, and give
that people a chance?

We are often met by the prejudicial proposal to
keep the Negro in his place. There can be no ob-

jection to this, provided we first give him a place to stay in. But to hinder, restrict, hedge, hamper, scorn, abuse, ridicule, and denounce should not, in all conscience, represent our relation to the race.

The questions herein discussed are those which appeal to clear and cool reason, and are not unworthy of the most studious consideration of even the highest and the best among us. Advantageous rootage will yield abundant fruitage.

CHAPTER IX.

A FORCE OF CONSERVATION.

It seems to have escaped the attention of writers on the subject of the Negro that that which is regarded as his weakest point of character is really his strongest, and one that has stood him in hand in the dire difficulties to which he has been subjected since his emancipation. The dominant characteristic of the Negro is that of submission, of tractableness. Nothing short of this possession could have saved the race from dissolution. Yet this trait has been often urged against the Negro as an indication of his weakness. In this event, his weakness is his strength. The stronger race has often taken advantage of this element of weakness, and in consequence, the Negro has been the sufferer, but he would have been a greater sufferer had he not possessed it. His refuge of protection in many an ordeal has been his quiet submissiveness to wrong, and then making the most of that which was left. Had the Negro been as aggressive as the white man, he would have been pulverized. He has met the repeated shocks of racial revolution with a resiliency that has saved his race from utter dissolution. This passive virtue has been his greatest means of conservation.

In this respect the Negro race has not been altogether unlike that of the Hebrew. This last-named race has been hounded through the centuries, without a land, without a language, and without laws, and yet has survived the shocks, revolutions and persecutions of the ages, and emerges into prominence with representative leaders in commerce, in politics, and in war, the greatest race the world has ever known. The American Negro is a new race which has been touched by the vitality of modern civilization, and is destined to play an important part in the history of the future in the states of America.

For centuries, Africa was the slave market of the world. The easy subserviency of the Negro together, with his muscularity and his power of endurance in hot climates, has been the occasion of his dissipation through the heated regions of the globe, but the flexibility of our republican institutions is aptly suited to the pliable character of the Negro, and it is here that he is coming to his own. Tendencies are always prophetic, and the indications are that the refluent influence of the American Negro will eventually prove the redemption of his dark fatherland. Into the realm of prediction, however, we need not now go.

It would have been difficult for any other race to have undergone that to which the Negro race has been subjected, without serious detriment, and yet the Negro has not only survived but has continued to thrive. With the patience of the ox he submitted to the hard and exacting demands of protracted bondage, and out of this passive disposition came the cheerfulness which lent song and melody to his labor on the hot plantations of the South, and made his gloomy quarters vibrant with joy at night when his heavy tasks of the day were done. Instead of the gloom and moroseness of almost any other people, the Negro injected a cheerful minstrelsy into his gloom, and drove dull care away. It is the testimony of travelers in Africa that the slaves of the Dark Continent accompany their tasks with song, just as do the Negroes in America. Gloomy and despairing indeed must be the condition of the Negro if he fails to give vent to melody. The gloomy cell so often his portion, the chain-gang on the street, the penal servitude on the plantation or in the penitentiary, stifle not his melody. He pines not over misfortune, as do other men, he broods not over calamity, he is not burdened with foreboding care as are others, he chafes not under smarting wrong, he cherishes no deeply-nourished grudge, but passively accepts the situation and is content to make the most of it, whatever it may be. By this means his strength is husbanded and when the opportunity is his, he is ready to seize it and press it on to his advantage.

Out of this disposition as a slave grew his devotion to his master. The severest punishment did not alienate his affection, and his subsequent jocularity would often disarm his owner of an ill-natured disposition toward him. To this same passive quality in the character of the Negro was the Southern Confederacy due for the success of its arms on the field. With no other race of men would this have proved true. But the Negro submitted against his well-known advantage, and it inured in several ways to his subsequent benefit. He did not accept freedom till it was literally thrust on him.

The period of his greatest disaster was when he was shunted off his accustomed plane of disposition and course of conduct, and was bewitched by unscrupulous whites into the political scrambles of the notorious reconstruction period. That which he then did was not really himself, but the schemes and designs of men of infamous purpose speaking through him as a subservient mouthpiece. Here the Negro was quite out of his element in an enforced aggression for which the dive and dramshop were largely responsible, and under the deception by which he was moved, he became the chief sufferer and the permanent burden-bearer of the ills of an infamous era.

But what of the efficacy of that passive quality of character since he has been subjected to dependence on his own resources? Has it stood him in hand during these years of sore trial since he has had to lean alone on himself? The Negro has never undertaken anything worthy without encountering difficulty and disadvantage. At every step of his progress his way has been disputed by obstructions of divers sorts. Many advantages have been denied him by his opponents. He has suffered not a little from a dominant and masterful prejudice. Pretexts and petty offenses have served as much to crowd our jails and penitentiaries as has genuine justice. Infliction on infliction has been borne with passive docility, and each recurring event has been suffered to pass into forgetfulness without opposition. Every possible advantage has been taken of the Negro in commercial transactions, of all of which he was duly aware, but he has quietly submitted and gone on his way. That passive disposition, docility of spirit, resiliency and adjustability of character have served as his shield of protection. Suppose he had been truculent and aggressive, he would have gone the way of the Indian— would have gradually disappeared from among men, at least in the states of America. Unpossessed of those strident qualities and burly passions which so often sway men in seasons of wrong, and which wear away efficiency and unpoise disposition, the Negro has, after each misfortune, taken up his march afresh with an alacrity of spirit that has been the astonishment of many.

Not that the Negro is lacking in assertion and persistency, but is of the quiescent cast. His coolness, cheerfulness, pliancy of disposition, and readiness of adjustment have prevailed where the more robust qualities would have failed. This quality of submissiveness on the part of the Negro has done more than he is aware of, in its appeal to the chivalric type of white manhood. *I*t has, not in a few instances, stirred into sympathy the depths of his white neighbors when resistance on his part would have failed, and aroused opposition. There is much of that in the genuine Anglo-Saxon which, to use the parlance of the street, is "for the under-dog in the fight." The weak and oppressed, the defenseless and dependent have never failed to appeal to the really chivalric white man. This was the very genius of the age of chivalry. *I*n more instances than the Negro is aware, heroic whites have stood between him and contemplated violence, simply because he was what he was as a defenseless and submissive being. His friends among the whites are the more numerous because of his possession of this quality.

While possessed of this docile spirit, the Negro, in his higher types is not wanting in pluck to grapple with difficulty, however forbidding, and by means of a combination of qualities so rare, he has largely succeeded. Back of much of his success has been the silent reinforcement of the better element of the whites. *I*t may seem a roundabout means of success, one of indirection, and certainly it is unusual, but by means of this quality the Negro has, in large measure, succeeded, and is destined yet more to succeed. Had the Negro been rebellious and assertive in the hour of his emancipation, he would never have succeeded in his subsequent course. His quiescent mood of temperament which so many have been swift to attribute to weakness, is the source of the Negro's strength, and will doubtless prove more a prevailing quality in the future than it has in the past.

While the Negro is timid and docile, it must not be presumed that he is lacking in a substratum of courage when occasion demands. It is an error to presume that the Negro is in the general acceptation of the term, a natural coward. Under conditions he will resist with desperate courage. Wherever his courage has been tested on the field of battle, he has proved himself an excellent soldier. It was a Federal commander who dispatched to Washington during the Civil War, concerning the Negro soldiers, "The colored troops fought nobly." The gallant charge of the Tenth Cavalry, a Negro troop, at San Juan Hill, is one of the events of the Spanish-American war.

But his staying quality is his subdued temperament. For his success, and it has been unique, he is more indebted to his docility of spirit than to any other cause. In a number of instances conditions have arisen which might have precipitated passion, but it has been held in abeyance till the storm has passed, and the Negro has quietly pursued his even way thenceforth. He has met misfortune without resistance, and yet with a strange, firm purpose

which sprang from the soil of his characteristic pas-
siveness, he has finally prevailed where often success
was not at all probable. Quietly dropping into the
current which was bearing the stronger race on to
success, and drifting, not aimlessly, but with a spirit
unperturbed, he was the more alive to the opportunities which came his way, and on these, as on buoys,
he has borne himself toward a destiny which grows
more luminous with his steady advancement.

The varied ordeals through which the Negro has
been compelled to pass since the coming of his freedom, have served to evoke this latent quality of his
character as the humdrum of slavery could not. In
slavery he was compressed within narrow bounds,
with no will of his own, and without personal choice
in the direction of his course; but as has been already remarked, this element, even then, was not
without avail. If it be accounted a weakness, how
happens it that the Negro has so marvelously succeeded in so many spheres? Weakness is not an
element of success. The truth of this paradoxical
condition is found in the fact that beneath this apparent weakness there is a hidden means of strength.
It is the preservation of an equanimity that seems
characteristic of the Negro race. Because of his
rare combination of qualities, the Negro has been
called, by some, an inscrutable being. This in-
scrutableness resides in the fact that he is capable
of wringing success at the most unconjectured quar-

ters, and at points where there was every indication of failure.

Left to himself, the Negro raises no tumults; incites no strikes; and when smitten, smites not again; when persecuted, bows to it in meekness; when wronged, seeks no malicious revenge, but peaceably goes his way and placidly dismisses it from his mind. Where others would resist, he tamely submits, and where others would cherish malice and hatred, he returns a quiet good humor.

Eliciting, as this does, the impulse of the old-time chivalry of the South, the Negro will find that in proportion as he establishes his genuine worth in his effort to improve, public opinion in his behalf will increase on the higher levels of the stronger race. This will serve to give him increased nerve, and fit him more to draw upward the lower elements of his race. The destiny of the Negro is within his own keeping. In proportion to his worth will it be recognized and appreciated. As time goes on, the duty of the family circle, the pulpit, and the school will become more pronounced, not only in holding that already gained, but in pressing with eager ambition and wisdom for a higher footing for the masses of the Negro race. Vagrancy must not only be discountenanced, but steadily overcome, and lawlessness, in all its forms, denounced. Each one gained to the higher round of progress and thrift, must become an evangel to win yet others. This seems to be the propelling spirit now animating the active moral forces of the race. Notwithstanding the disorders on the lower levels, and they are destined yet to continue, at least for a season, the race is on the onward march. *It* is making vaster opportunities for itself each year. Much has been most creditably done within the space of a few years, but much more remains to be done. One thing at least has been established by the leaders of the race, and that is the proof that the Negro has capabilities which years ago he was not supposed to possess. His route to success has been an anomalous one, but, in the end, it is genuine success.

So long as the race remained prostrate and helpless, it was regarded as a menace to the South, but this bugaboo is rapidly disappearing, as the Negro becomes identified with the interests of a common country, and is a contributor to its usefulness and its wealth. That which has been done by some, can be done by many. Those who have succeeded show the possibility of success to others. Pioneers are prophets. Forerunners are necessary in all great movements and undertakings. But leaders are, after all, only leaders. They point the way, indicate the direction to be followed, and press toward the heights, but if they are to advance, or even hold their own, they must be consistently reinforced. That there is a slow but assuring racial reaction in

process in the South seems clear. The growing
worthiness of the Negro, his outreach of enterprise,
his interest in current affairs, so far as he is permitted to share in them, and above all, his placid
temperament are serving to bring him into closer
touch with the stronger race. The movements of
the Negro are closely watched, not so much with a
critical spirit, as with one of interest and concern,
and his worthy deeds make a profound impression.
There never was a happier conception for the race
than that of the organization of the National Negro
Business League, which meets annually in some portion of the country. It focuses and summarizes
the achievements of the Negro, calls attention to his
expanding usefulness, and is conducted with so
much saneness and remarkable judgment, that it is
winning annually increasing attention.

There can be no denial of the fact that where a
Negro has made himself at all conspicuous, no matter in what community in the South, he is esteemed
by all whose esteem is of any worth. Just in proportion as he shows himself worthy as an American,
a citizen, a civilizer, and an upright man of affairs,
he will receive cordiality of welcome at the hands
of the stronger race. Can he ask for more? In
truth, this demand will act more and more for the
elevation of the race. If a standard is erected to
which he can even measurably bring himself, he is
the beneficiary far more than the white man.

The outlook is, then, one of inspiration for the Negro race. There are yet obstructions many, and certain species of injustice to be corrected, but time will take care of these, and the calm poise of the race is doing more to effect this than any other agency.

CHAPTER X.

NEGRO WOMANHOOD.

A race or nation is just as good as its women—no better. Whether on the highest plane to which a people may have attained in the scale of excellence, or the lowest to which one may be depressed, the principle admits of equal application. In every age, under all conditions, the fact remains—woman is the arbiter of the destiny of a people.

For the reason of this we do not have far to go to ascertain. Woman is the embodied home, and the home is the basis of all institutions, the buttress of society. The primal form of government, the home, holds its regnant place in the society of the world. It is the fountain source of power and influence, of character and sentiment, and has lent a dominant color to every great historic event, every movement that has upheaved in the revolutions of time. The mother and wife are the vital source of power in the home. That accumulated and mysterious influence is the leaven which has lifted and expanded, or the element which has contracted and shriveled, in proportion to the character of woman. The lesson of the position providentially assigned to the sex has never been lost to the world.

No less applicable is the principle to the Negro race in the phenomenal transition through which it has been passing since the freedom of '65. Of the unfortunate effects on the condition of the race of Negroes in the uncontrolled animalism of the men of the dominant race, we of the South know perfectly well. To the slave, the white man was the highest ideal, and the conduct of thousands of them had a most untoward effect on the character of Negro womanhood. The trespass of the stronger on the weaker, the advantage taken of the relations between the owner and the slave, as well as that of other representatives of the controlling race, the levelling of differences by clandestine conduct, which has not ceased with the years subsequent to emancipation, have left, and still leave, an influence for evil in the minds of the colored women. If they shared in the fault by reason of the weakness occasioned first by the laxness of original savagery, and as a result of the examples of slave life, what shall be said of the white man with ages of cultivated restraint behind him? It is just this condition which excites the apprehension, so often voiced in half-suppressed utterance, of race amalgamation. The interdiction of intermarriage between the two races in the states in which the Negroes are massed, serves as a ban and barrier, so far as legal statute is concerned, and raises an insurmountable partition between the races. This meets alike the approbation of both races, but does not serve as a check to the vice on the lower levels of life.

The hope of the Negro as a people lies in the growing aspiration of his leaders to preserve intact the integrity of the race. Nor is this the least among the difficult tasks of the race, which in their aggregate are manifold. In this endeavor these leaders encounter a vice which is rooted deep into the ages, the growth of which was not retarded under the regime of slavery. They must needs teach the alphabet of chastity under discouraging conditions. In the delicate assumption they must necessarily reach the wills, the consciences, and the loyal race pride of their young womanhood. The initial sources of influence on which they must rely must be the home, the church, the school. Rigid safeguards must be placed above the persons of their growing womanhood. Chaste womanhood for the Negro, as well as for every other race, is indispensable if the race, as such, is to be preserved. Virtue must be the angel with flaming sword, guarding first of all the portals of the home. More than anything else, yea, more than all things else combined, must be the moral strength of Negro womanhood. This is the one indispensable first stone laid in the foundation of race integrity, and no less the cement and the final capstone of the whole. The protection of the womanliness of woman in the Negro race is the bulwark of Negro race integrity.

*I*f there were nothing else now before the race—**if**
all other questions were already settled concerning
the biracial difficulty in the South, industrial, social,
political, educational—and all of these are far from
reduction to an undisturbed basis—and this solitary
question of Negro womanhood remained, it were
amply sufficient within itself, to enlist the profound-
est moral concern of both races. *I*n its very nature
it is the one fundamental question, the one crowning
concern. There is no disposition in a matter so
transcendentally important to evade the brunt of the
issue, nor to do other than to treat the case as it deserves. *I*n grappling with a question the proportions of which are so fundamental and colossal, it
would be the utmost recreancy to duty to be other
than candid.

There is profound philosophy in the pronounced
guidance given the race, first of all, in the realm of
industry. The moral side of this course exceeds
far that of the economic. The first vision of thousands of Negroes in their emergence from the bonds
of slavery was that of deliverance from toil. To
such, freedom was synonymous of idleness. Hap-
pily, this was not true of many other thousands
among them, and from the class uninfluenced by a
delusion so fatal, came the practical leaders of the
race who taught the lesson that industry, and not
the veneer of scholarship and a showy appearance,
is the first essential of race respectability if not of
race preservation. It was the embodiment of this

thought in the founding of the greatest Negro institution in the world that made President Booker T. Washington the greatest Negro in the world. It was not alone an answer to the empty dream of idleness, it is the piston by means of which a multitudinous people are moving to a more advanced position. The chief difficulty, then, being the largely unchecked unchastity reaching from the influence of original savagery clear through the blighting conditions of slavery, this serious difficulty to race preservation would have received fresh incentive by the mistaken notion of the real meaning of emancipation, but for the timely action of certain wise leaders. Idleness is one of the chief causes of immorality among women, no matter what the race or nation be, the climate, or the condition. When to the blight already named, is superinduced that of idleness, it becomes a question of growing formidableness to the women of the Negro race. Hence the wisdom of the inculcation of principles of industry and thrift so abundantly illustrated in the Negro industrial schools in the states of the South.

To leave this branch of the subject here would be manifestly unfair to the Negro race. Among his other aspirations is to be named that of a higher ideal of character. The higher plane of the racial life of the Negro is being constantly supplemented by fresh installments of strength. Each year the racial ranks at the front are being reinforced by men and women of undoubted moral strength.

Along the heights are the exceptional ones of exalted worth who serve as a source of inspiration to the struggling masses beneath. Actuated by a purpose to make the race worthy of a place on the American continent, so fundamental a principle as that of chaste and pure womanhood is not lost sight of. That this spirit is growing, and that the race is rising in the scale of moral excellence on the side of both sexes is one of the most assuring indications of the worthiness of the race. Infractions of race integrity decrease as the gradations of Negro character are followed from the low levels until they cease on the higher planes of racial life. There is an evident race patriotism, a commendable loyalty looking to a wholesome segregation of blood, that is growing with the growth of the race. Without all this, all else that is claimed for Negro advancement were a sham.

Not until the Negro was free did he come to know the full meaning of home. He had a habitation in the hut of his servitude, but not a home. To him a home was an institution as new practically as his freedom was to him novel. Mother and wife were largely mere names, so far as their influence for practical good to the millions of the enslaved race went. In starting on his other tasks on a race career, the Negro had to found the new idea of home, and begin at bottom to generate the principles of home life. Among the accomplishments of the race, this achievement, silently but certainly wrought into the texture of the Negro life of the South, is not the least. To hundreds of thousands of the race, home now has a meaning, and mother and wife are no longer practical misnomers. Severed families and disrupted homes were common in the traffic of slavery. This destroyed the true sense of security in the attempted home in the Negro quarters of the Long Ago, and individualized the Negro in such a way as to blot out the idea of home.

The commendable ambition of the Negro to own land and to build a home of his own, each as good as his means will allow, is one of the most animating signs of Negro progress. A race possessed of an ambition like this, and exemplifying a spirit such as is shown by the Negro race at present, is not certainly on the decline. All this circles around the single idea of womanhood, for at last, the Negro woman is the Negro home. A race which supplements its ambition to attain to learning, to commercial and realty possession, to schools and churches of excellence, with that of building and maintaining a comfortable home, is not among the decadent peoples. Measured by the ambition alone of founding the best homes possible, the Negro race would be regarded as on the up-grade. When this is reinforced by a group of ambitions that ramify into professional, industrial, and educational life, the progress of the Negro race must be regarded as indisputable.

Like other assets of the Negro, this improved

home is annually increasing, alike in the city and in the country. *I*n many of them are to be found the elements which elevate and inspire—books, magazines, musical instruments, pictures and paintings, together with decorations graduated, of course, by the means of the owner. This generation of home owners will be immensely increased when the families of boys and girls, issuing from conditions of a higher conception of life, shall themselves take their places in the future onward career of the race. In cooperation with the home other agencies are, meanwhile, active in the production of young manhood and womanhood—the schools in their annual products, the aspiring class reaching to heights above them, the elimination of the saloon from the states of the South, and other agencies by the activity of which the race is being steadily aided in its ambitious march. Still, the disparity between the chaste and the others is so great as to be well-nigh appalling, and would be to any other race than that of one which has resisted disintegration under the most adverse conditions possible. There is a long and fearful uphill struggle still ahead of the Negro race, and from one point of view, its environment of temptation from low, seductive white sources is against it. In some particulars, the inertia seems almost irresistible, and the friend of the Negro would be almost tempted to lose heart, but for the inherent genius of the worthy colored man to overcome appalling discouragements. With undaunted step he has entered the various pursuits and professions, and while often ridiculed and discouraged, he has increasingly vindicated his right to live, to labor and to prosper.

There are serious local difficulties in some parts of the South where traditional influences operate to the degradation of Negro women, to say nothing of the effects on the class of men who are largely responsible for these conditions. In sections, especially where the "sporting gentry" prevail, Negro womanhood is peculiarly exposed to imposition. But the steady progress of the Negro is serving to expose these more and more, and with the same commendable zeal displayed for a higher life, these influences must eventually succumb. So little is generally known of the silent and interior agencies at work among the higher class of Negroes, and so much is known of the opposite class, as the eye of the public is directed chiefly to this lower class, that the public generally is altogether unaware of the contributions which the worthier Negro is making to our common welfare. One must be familiar with these interior conditions, and consider them in their totality before he is able to pass proper judgment on the Negro as a whole. To know of the strenuous efforts of thousands of worthy men and women among them, of the force of their example for good to the public, of the sacrifices which they are constantly making for the elevation of their kind, is to awaken the liveliest hope and inspire thankfulness. Detached facts are occasionally brought to light respecting Negro progress, but they are often regarded as so exceptional as to indicate nothing else than exceptionalness. A fair presentation of the meritoriousness of the race would awaken profound surprise. Not only in the attainment of better material things is the Negro laboring, but for higher ideals of character he is also striving.

But the cardinal hope of the race resides in its womanliness. That many of the men of the race have made a definite advance, affording a magnet to attract others upward, is immensely to their credit, and that the educated class of young women is doing much to segregate their race on an independent basis by the preservation of their womanly honor, is worthy of all praise. If no other considerations were urged in favor of the scholastic training of the Negro, the fact that as they are educationally trained they become more numerously virtuous and more segregated as a race, would be sufficient to prompt every patriot to espouse the cause of his education and elevation. Here as elsewhere may it not be said that because the Negro has advanced so far in the womanly uplift of the race, and in the establishment of homes, in the face of abounding disadvantage, that we may look for a rapid increase of these in the years of the immediate future?

If on the men of the race there is imposed a duty of clearing the way for the future progress of their people, on the women of the Negro race is imposed a work more silent and less spectacular, but of the highest importance in the stimulation of virtue and the safeguarding of their younger sisters against the pitfalls of the times and the peculiar perils of their environment. That there is the utmost endeavor and care on the part of thousands of Negro mothers and wives to rectify conditions and to fortify the young womanhood of the race against the dangers of prevailing vice, is true. The extent of prevalent vice in the years of the past, and the ruin which it has wrought, have served to quicken the diligence and care of these worthy women, in bringing into requisition the brace of moral forces, which without these previous conditions would not now be so earnestly emphasized. The laxness of past years is suggesting greater restrictions in the present, just as the dangers laid bare by the past now show the conditions to be shunned. The Negro woman must vindicate her sex in the matter of chastity, just as the race of which they are an important part, has already come to vindicate itself against the charge originally made of racial incapacity. The encouragement of this feature of Negro endeavor, on the part of the whites, would be most praiseworthy. Genuine womanliness is so fundamental to the preservation of a race that it cannot be accorded a secondary place in the movement toward loftier ideals on the part of the Negro.

CHAPTER XI.

The Christian public of America is confronted by a condition which is unique in the history of nations. Briefly stated, it is that a segment of the African race has been forced from its haunts in the land of its nativity, brought to America, subjected to bondage for centuries, set at liberty, given the right of the franchise, and then, without experience, without initial wisdom, and without means of a livelihood, left to care for itself. The complications growing out of these conditions we call the Negro problem. That it is a problem centering in the Negro, by reason of the successive steps already named, there is no doubt, but if it be the Negro problem, it is by no means the Negro's problem. If he be the agent by which it has been created, he is not its creator. It is the creation of others with the Negro as an humble instrument. If the problem be in consequence of the Negro, it is nevertheless the problem of the white man. To solve it is, therefore, the duty of the whites. Nor will its solution be without the amplest compensation, for in making the Negro all that he is capable of becoming, the white man, by this same exercise, will himself be made the better and greater. In making the Negro he will make himself.

Nor is the problem one for the white man of the South alone, it is a national question. It is quite popular, even in certain high official circles, without the states of the South, for some to say, "It is a Southern question, and let the people of the South settle it. They have the Negro on their hands, understand him, and they only can control the situation." Yet it is neither a Southern question, nor yet is it a Northern one, but one the settlement of which must be made by the people of the whole country. The results of the labor of the Negro were shared in alike by the people of all the nation, and were being vastly enjoyed in the East even during the long period of the abolition agitation. For years together, while the abolition tide ran high, the cotton mills of the East were manufacturing the fabrics from the cotton fields of the South, to the enrichment even of those who were loudest in their protestations against slavery. This is said not by way of recrimination, but as a matter of fact, and in maintenance of the statement that all shared in the products of the toil of the slave, and to that degree, at least, are under obligation to participate in his present relief.

The South has not been altogether recreant to the obligation imposed by the continued retention of the Negro within her borders. With her fields left desolate by a protracted war, her industrial system wrecked, her people demoralized and impoverished, the South has been compelled to provide educational facilities for the Negro along with provisions for the children of the whites. A double obligation has thus been imposed under conditions when the South was least prepared to assume it. These educational facilities have been altogether inadequate, but there have continued, in the South, annual appropriations for a cause so meritorious. True, there has not been lacking on the part of some from without the South, a commendable display of beneficence in behalf of the education of the Negro, but even with this, there is still an alarming inadequacy of means.

For forty-five years this condition has continued to exist. At the outset, in the dawn of Negro freedom, there were practically four and a half million illiterates among the Negroes. Practically that same number exists today. Illiteracy has been immensely reduced, but the colored race has also immensely increased, so that the situation in the South, so far as the number of Negro illiterates is concerned, is about that which it was in 1865. The Negro has made gigantic strides in the advancement of his race; he has done what he could, and has done it well, and has surpassed the most sanguine expectations of his friends, South and North, by his commendable feats; still, the means for his education have been altogether inadequate.

While it might be said that the states of the South have not done all that might have been done for the education of the Negro, that which has been done, has been done out of her poverty, and that she should have done as much is praiseworthy. The condition is one which appeals not to the South alone, in behalf of an unfortunate race, but to all the states alike. It is a question which addresses itself to the constructive statesmanship of a Christian nation. There is little hesitation to appropriate millions annually to internal improvements, to public buildings, and the improvement of waterways, and the increase of the navy, not to act so much for public defense as to act as a defiance to an imaginary "yellow peril," while the great black peril is statedly overlooked, and is not even so much as named. Nor is it forgotten that there is a white peril, in the illiterate Caucasions in the states of the South. Education is as much in demand for the one as for the other. This is a condition left largely untouched for long and dreary decades by the Christian nation of America.

Not alone from this has the Negro population of the South suffered. The question of his education has not been without stout opposition locally. It is claimed by not a few in the South, that from the education of the Negro there would ensue a worse condition than that which comes of his being kept in a state of ignorance. This objection to the education of a certain class is not new. It was urged long ago against Christianizing the Negro of the West Indies, when the Moravian missionaries, Dober and Nitzschmann, sought that far region to carry the gospel to the Negro slaves laboring on the sugar plantations. To the Moravians belong the honor of first preaching the gospel to the enslaved Negro. Enlightenment was opposed because it was stoutly insisted that it would permanently unfit the slave for profitable service. The same monstrous objection confronted William Carey when he went to *I*ndia with the gospel. The English traders resisted him by cruel insult and mistreatment because it was claimed that the enlightenment of the people of *I*ndia would render them the more capable of resisting the cupidity imposed on them by the avaricious British. The time was when the education of women in England was opposed for a similar reason—that by the diversion of the faculties of woman to literary pursuits she would be unfitted for domestic cares and household duties. It was this agitation in England which evoked from the pen of the celebrated wit, Sydney Smith, in *The Edinburgh Review*, a scathing article on female education, who, among other things said: "Can anything be more absurd than to suppose that the care and solicitude which a mother feels for her children depends upon her ignorance of Greek and mathematics? It would appear from such objections, that ignorance is the great civilizer of the world."

Not until it can be demonstrated that ignorance is more helpful than education, is the objection worthy of serious consideration. As a matter of fact, there are thousands of educated Negroes in America. Has the country suffered in consequence? With their increasing efficiency as a result of mental training there has been a corresponding increase of prosperity. Does prosperity invite detriment? Is increased skill in the use of implements of husbandry and of the shop to be decried in the clamor for ignorant labor?

But the objection to the Negro does not end here. Years ago he was mocked with the charge of incapacity, and now that he has shown himself capable, the cry is raised from the opposite quarter that he is becoming a competitor in the varied spheres of labor. Without stopping to show the utter futility of an outcry like this, because of the multiplicity of the means of labor, and because of the sufficiency of room for all, yet it may be said that the Negro in his onward strides may expect to encounter this difficulty. In proportion to the growth of his efficiency will he continue to encounter opposition of divers kinds. In the erection of the barrier already named, there are involved unjustifiable opposition, the attempted retard of a race which is seeking to advance, and to promote its interests, the attempted check of industry, the effort to take advantage of a people whose conditions place them at a disadvantage, an unworthy appeal to racial prejudice, and the effort to crowd the Negro off the scene altogether.

Looking still further into the situation, every one is aware of numerous acts of unkindness, petty in-

justice, and not infrequently of cruelty, and yet
oftener than otherwise these occur without the
slightest provocation. A single incident will serve
to illustrate many others. Some time ago, in a
Southern city, a street car was in the act of starting
from a terminal point which was near a railway station. Between the two points the sand was deep, the
sun was blazing, and the interval of distance un-
shaded. The hand of the conductor of the street car
was already on the bell cord, when he standing in a
group of young men on the rear platform, observed a
corpulent Negro man with a heavy bundle over his
shoulder, and a large, worn sachel in his hand, tug-
ging as rapidly as he could through the hot deep sand
to reach the street car. He was evidently a passenger
seeking transfer across the city. The struggles of
the black man, his strained eyes and perspiring face,
excited the merriment of the group on the platform,
in which merriment the conductor joined. Just as
the Negro came within a few feet of the car the
bell was rung and the car started. With desperate
efforts the struggling man was enabled to swing his
heavy bundle to the platform, but with his satchel
he was left rapidly behind. A block or two further
on the bundle was kicked into the street, leaving the
unfortunate man widely separated from a portion of
his luggage. Under similar conditions a white man
would have resorted to the courts for redress, but
what recourse was possibly left the Negro? Expressions of injustice, not to say of downright in-

humanity, like this, are not infrequent, and call for the protection of a loftier sentiment. Not alone by the expression of sentiment, but by the exercise of direct interest and effort should the Negro be aided. In the providence of God there is committed to our care, as common trustees, the fate of millions of people. Independent of the obligations imposed for reasons stated in a former chapter, is the one of bare humanity. Had the Negro never struck an industrial blow, nor yielded a cent of profit, and was still in contact with the stronger and more highly favored race, the demand of Christian humanitarianism would still be urgent. But that which he has been to the country, that of which he has been the producer, together with that which he now is, a receptive, responsive man, groping his way as best he can toward a better life and condition— all these would seem to indicate that he is worthier of something more than aversion and prejudice.

Side by side with the white race, the large Negro population affords a sphere for the exercise of the spirit both of home and foreign missions. Africa is at our door—Ethiopia stretches forth her hands. The misinterpretation of providence would seem, under existing conditions, to be impossible. If, however, our thoughts concerning the Negro be only those of opposition, prejudice or aversion, then shall we absolutely fail of the appreciation of our duty.

We despise the arrogance and exclusiveness of a sect which flourished in the days of the Master, the haughty bearing of which sect was such that it abstained from touching others, fearful of contamination. We detest the stateliness of their port as they held themselves aloof from the Gentiles, whom they classed as heathen, and whose bearing wore the expression, "*I* am better than thou." We read with interest of the prejudice of a Jewish disciple who had been commissioned to a Gentile heathen home, and who after a struggle was compelled to say, "Of a truth, I perceive that God is no respecter of persons." With reluctant spirit the stern Jew yielded, and the centurion was recognized as a man of God purely from unclouded principle.

Far more than we are willing to acknowledge, we are swayed by prejudice. While its class among the passions is that of the unworthy, prejudice is as strong as steel, as firm as adamant. *I*n its stability it is like the mountains. *I*n its paradoxical character it can both hear and not hear. Deaf to a thousand thunders on one side, on the other it can hear the tick of a watch. An element of weakness, there is yet nothing stronger. While it is unworthy, it is one of the most potent of the agencies that sway the judgment. *I*t excites ridicule and opposition where it should stir pity and awaken interest. But once overcome by judgment and conscience, it is like the sudden reversal of a mountain torrent. Saul, the prejudiced Pharisee, became Paul, the prince of apostles. *I*t indicates the sudden development of a great character when prejudice succumbs to principle, and passion yields to duty.

This is the demand of the present hour. More than on any others Christianity has laid its grip on the white race of the world, yet innately this white race cherishes an aversion for the colored races—the red, the tawny, the saffron, and the black. This aversion is born of nature, not of grace. If God is no respecter of persons, neither should his people be. Controlled as we may be by the conventionalities of social life, with God, the common basis is one of humanity. And the genius of our Christianity is one of religious equality. Not till the middle wall of partition is leveled religiously between man and man, and every nation and tribe is greeted on the basis of cofraternity, will the religion of the Nazarene make headway in the world. The enlarged application of this principle to the present discussion is unnecessary, its statement is its application. More than on any ground, Christianity halts just here. No Christian can follow alone the cleavage of preference, for that may be only the index-finger of prejudice; each must yield to duty and principle if his convictions savor of the views of the Nazarene. "Let every man be fully persuaded in his own mind."

The numerous inequalities in the application of the laws of a common country; the frequent injustices already recited in the preceding pages; the acts of vengeance indulged and tolerated, and the neglect of the moral condition of millions of a race, no matter what be the reasons given or the pretext offered, are conditions which call for white Christian manliness, sympathy, and effort. *I*t should be clear to all alike that present conditions are bearing on their surface toward the future, the seeds of troubles to come. The results are not yet visible, they are only indicated in the tendencies of the present, and tendencies are prophetic. Unless relief to the present situation be afforded, a harvest of problematical difficulties will grow for a future generation. Nothing is clearer than that demoralization is insidiously seeking its way beneath the foundations of our most cherished institutions. Remove from the present generation respect for law and a disregard of the simplest rights, and the vision of disaster already looms on the horizon of the future.

Some time ago the writer was seated in the editorial room of a certain prominent daily journal, when the report was brought in that a young man known to the editor had killed a Negro, and the reporter of the deed said, "And he is thinking of running off." The reply from the young editor was: "Not for killing a Negro!" The conditions from which sentiments like these are even possible portend nothing cheering for the future. If the sturdy Christian sentiment of the land cannot correct these and other conditions, nothing can.

CHAPTER XII.

MOB VIOLENCE.

(For much of the substance of this chapter, the author acknowledges his indebtedness to that admirable and incisive work of Edgar Gardner Murphy, entitled "The Present South," Chapter VI.)

Until a late period in the history of the South, lynching was practically unknown. There was an occasional outbreak of violence, but so rare was it, that it excited unusual surprise and comment, and created a profound sensation. But within the last few decades of Southern history, lynching has become so prevalent that it ceases now to excite horror or to awaken surprise. Like all other evils with which society is afflicted, and which remain unchecked, lynching has continued to grow until it has come to assume alarming proportions. Like other unchecked evils, too, lynching has passed its original bounds, not now being restricted to the infliction of violent death for a single crime, but employed for other offenses, sometimes for the most trivial. Nor are its victims of one race now, as was once true. Once only Negroes were executed by the mob, but it has come to pass, as a result of the growth of the evil, whites have become its victims also.

With respect to lynching, it is as true as it is of

all open violations of the law—lawlessness begets lawlessness. Tolerated and unrestrained, lawlessness invariably grows. The essence of lynching is not the satisfaction of the law, but revenge, and revenge is an endless chain. For the same reason which first actuates it, it may be continued indefinitely. Once sought, it may be responded to with the same motive, and thus continue indefinitely. *I*ts direct effect is demoralization without limit. No law can be satisfied by the display of revenge.

Justification for lynching is sought upon these grounds, the first of which is that the methods which it employs are necessary to prevent the repetition of the crime of which the criminal is guilty. The second ground is to avoid the delay of court procedure in the matter of bringing the perpetrator to trial. The third is to save the victim of assault from the humiliation of publicity in bearing testimony at the trial of the offender. That is to say, this was the original basis when lynching was employed alone for criminal assault. But the demoralization produced by the methods founded on these grounds as a common basis has long since passed beyond these boundaries, and has assumed a vaster range in which sometimes even petty offenses are included.

By even a casual examination of the basis of the mob bent on lynching, we shall find that the grounds sought for its justification are altogether untenable—that they fall far short in each instance of the original purpose. Take, for instance, the first-named reason assigned—that of preventing the repetition of the crime. Has lynching done this? Do the offenders against the law decrease because of mobocrary? Has it proved a remedy for the crime of rape? Every one knows that it has not acted as a deterrent to crime. No matter how this may be accounted for, it is true. The holocaust of crime continues, the demoralization is still rampant, the law continues to be violated. This has been evident for years, and yet the practice of lynching continues. Is there not evidence in this that the plea of the lynchers is not sincere when they claim that it is to prevent the repetition of the deed, and does it not go far toward establishing the fact that it is in the interest of revenge, rather than for the purpose named as the reason for the mob?

How about the law's delay in the trial of offenders? There is occasional reason for this complaint, but not often with respect to crime committed, especially by those who are charged with assault on women. There are conditions when the offense against a given victim is peculiarly horrible, and when the offender, as a member of a weaker race, becomes the object of special public wrath, and when the courts seem tardy of action. Beneath the restlessness evinced on such occasions it is the spirit of revenge which cries for execution, and not the spirit of justice for which the populace clamors. The crowd on the outside has already rendered the verdict, and demands the penalty, and yet, not a step has been taken save that of the apprehension of the offender. Under a strain of popular excitement and exasperation, a short time is regarded as quite long. Delays of the court do not ordinarily come in connection with "cases where the accused is a helpless and ignorant member of society, but where the defense can command those resources of legal talent and of technical procedure which are possible only to the rich."* Where are the cases on record where heinous crime in any of the states has failed of prompt action on the part of the courts? It does not seem that a charge like this can be justly made against our American judiciary. As between the morbid mob, swayed solely by passion, and a court where justice is sought to be administered, there should be no hesitation of choice.

The plea sometimes made that the mob is "the people" resuming their power delegated to the court, is too flimsy as a defense, and utterly void of the thing assumed. So far from being "the people," the mob is usually composed of an irresponsible minority with nothing of popular coherency holding it together, nothing of a great popular and permanent movement for good, utterly nothing to vindicate its existence or its conduct, and going to pieces after the excitement is past. Think of a body of reckless men "assuming the august prerogatives of society!"

So far from being "the people," every mob is an enemy of the people assailing the strongest cordon of defense about society. It turns law into chaos,

*"The Present South," p. 178.

and deliberately sets at naught the most cherished institutions of the people. It usurps the most delicate functions possible, and for order substitutes violence, to avoid which the courts are established and maintained. Into the hands of the police, or the constabulary, and the courts is lodged the apprehension and proper adjudication of offenses against society, and these are the strongholds really attacked by the mob. In the protection of that most sacred of all earthly boons, human life, on the one hand, and of society against crime, on the other, the constabulary and court are maintained. They, one or both, may err, sometimes do, but they are the nearest approximation possible to the ends in view. To protect the innocent, and to punish the guilty, each with due deliberation, is the function of the court. Its duty is clear and well-defined. That there may be no undue delay, and equally no undue haste, should be the motive controlling the court.

At times there has seemed to be unseemly haste in the trials of offenders charged with the crime of assault on women. Courts have been hurriedly called, juries empanelled, the verdict rendered, and the sentence pronounced within the space of a few hours. Under conditions like these, with the public mind inflamed, the verdict has been made in advance, and the court procedure has been nothing more than a merely mechanical performance. There is danger, under conditions like these, as Mr. Murphy wisely suggests, in his "Present South," of seeking to prevent the mob from turning itself into a court by turning the court into a mob. The animus of at least some mobs has been shown by their forcibly taking prisoners from the officers after they have been duly tried, convicted, and sentenced, and while passing from the court-room to the prison, have been hanged in utter defiance of the law before the eyes of jurors and court alike. What becomes of the pretense of the protection of society in view of a spectacle like this? Fortunately for society, these morbid minorities are quite anything else than the representatives of the sentiments of "the people." Criminality like this is at least as harmful to the interests of society as is that of the individual charged with the crime for which he was sentenced to hang.

Coming now to the last pretext offered in defense of mobocracy—that of protecting the victim of the crime from being forced publicly to face her accuser in the court, this is as devoid of substantiation as are the other grounds over which we have come. By reason of its association, and that a woman, or a feminine child, this has been considered unanswerable when urged in defense of the existence of the mob. To quote again Mr. Murphy, in the "Present South," there may be said in reply to this: "yet when we have eliminated the cases—by far the greater number—in which the prisoner of the mob was not even charged with any crime against women, but with arson, or robbery, or attempted murder, and when we have eliminated, among the cases of assault among women, the number in which death has resulted, and the victim is thus prevented from all testimony, legal or extra-legal, the number of cases which come within the traditional excuse is extremely small." That on which the argument in defense of the mob is founded, then, is the ordeal of bearing testimony in the court, and thus add humiliation to shame and criminal injury by being exposed afresh to public gaze. But is the woman really relieved of this ordeal by the mob? Is she not more exposed to publicity than she would be in a trial held under restrictions such as are guaranteed the court? Let us see.

The judge before whom the trial is held has full authority to clear the court-room of all excepting those directly interested. He has authority to confine the examination to questions which occasion no offense, or in his discretion, so change the place of holding the court as to preserve the utmost privacy, and yet secure the ends of justice. Is there any such guardianship of privacy in the home of the victim where any one, or every one, who wishes to join in the promiscuous crowd in the scout of the country, arresting every suspected Negro and haling him into her presence is permitted to enter? Not one suspected criminal, perhaps, but a number are brought by the miscellaneous multitude before her for identification. So much for the protection of privacy from prurient curiosity.

How about the identification? *Is* one able always to say, "Thou art the man?" In her darkened room can the victim say positively who is or who is not the assailant? In a number of reported instances, victims have said that they could not positively say that the apprehended Negro was the one who made the assault, yet, in its fury, this same mob of excited men, these chivalrous protecters of society, these who call themselves "the people," have assumed that a certain one is the criminal assailant, and, acting on this assumption, have hanged him. Supposing that the arrested one be the assailant, there is not a stiva of right guaranteed the violent crowd to inflict punishment. On the most slender circumstantial evidence sometimes, mobs have acted in the execution of their deeds. What is the result of all this?

The law has been violently violated by the mob; the public demoralized; the courts abjured, and the relations between the races made more stringent without cause.

The mob is without a single redeeming quality. It has everything in it to condemn, nothing to commend. *I*t may have its defenders, but it has no defense. The end which it serves is hurtful and only hurtful. The recognition of the fact that this pseudo-chivalry deals a blow at society at large is sufficient within itself for heroic steps to be taken to give a summary check to this barbarous practice. It is this growing public sense which found a voice in "The (Atlanta) Constitution," under date of June 27th, 1903, when it says: "The time when the lynching of a certain breed of brutes could be winked at because of satisfaction that punishment came to him quietly and to the uttermost, has given way to a time when the greater peril to society is the mob itself which does the work of vengeance. Against the growth of that evil the best sense of the nation needs to combine and enforce an adequate protection."*

Later than this came a recommendation in a message to Congress from President Roosevelt that the matter be made one of national import by the passage of a law against lynching by Congress. These omens point to a gradual cessation of the crime of lynching by virtue of the robust public sentiment of the people of the country at large. Nothing is clearer than that lynching must claim attention such as it has not hitherto had. The able journalism of the South is becoming more pronounced against it, but this is not sufficient of itself to check it. The appeal comes to the highest type of patriotism to wipe out a stain which has become national in its effect, though restricted largely to only one part of the American Union.

It is refreshing in this connection to present an editorial from the columns of *The Courier-Journal*,

*Quoted from "The Present South," p. 182.

Louisville, Kentucky, under date Aug. 13th, 1909.
*I*t is as follows:

"THE COLOR LINE."

"The color line is drawn sharply by lynching in
Kentucky. Several weeks ago a Frankfort Negro
was lynched by a mob for having shot a circus man.
In Trigg county, a Negro boy, charged with attempted assault, was lynched. Between the dates of
these two lynchings Dr. Nuttall, a physician in
charge of patients at the 'Feeble Minded *I*nstitute,'
at Frankfort, was charged with having assaulted a
woman under his care. He was allowed ample time
to make preparation to avoid arrest, and after a good
deal of delay that might easily have been avoided,
a reward was offered for him. There was no apparent interest upon the part of the authorities in
bringing him to trial.

"The hoodlums at Frankfort and those in Trigg
county committed murder for the pleasure there was
in stringing up a defenseless victim. The three
brothers of the girl in Trigg county, to whom an
improper proposal was made, were guarding the
Negro on his way to jail, when the mob interfered.
Their conduct under trying circumstances was creditable. The Negro no doubt would have been convicted if he had been put in jail. A Negro tried for
criminal assault is not dealt tenderly with by a jury
of white men.

"There is but one conclusion to be drawn from the three cases. Attempted criminal assault is punishable by death without trial, if the accused be black. Shooting and wounding is punishable by death without trial, if the accused is black. Criminal assault is to be winked at, if the accused is white and prominent. It is difficult to decide which is more humiliating to decent citizens, the mob murders or the contemptible machinery of the law which admits of courtesy being shown to Dr. Nuttall."

Yet in the face of these facts, we hear much about the Negroes shielding their criminals from justice. It seems eminently proper for the authorities to fumble about matters provided the criminal be not of a given color. No serious protest is raised if one who is not a Negro be furnished avenues of escape from the consequences of his crime, much of which proves, not so much the desire to bring the criminal, irrespective of all considerations, to justice, as that of the disappointment of the mob to find its victim in order to wreak on him its full vengeance.

This is said, not to encourage the Negro to shield his victim from justice, nor in the least to justify it, but in the interest of the protection of society against all criminals, no matter what their color or position be. If it be wrong for the Negro to protect the criminal, it is equally so for every other to do so. In any event, it is the principle of *particeps criminis*. No system of society is safe, nor can it endure, where any class is depressed and suppressed on account of any disorder or criminality, while another is supported and upheld for the same, the authorities meanwhile abetting. These conditions in our Southern society cannot be condoned. They create a gap that is widening with time, and sooner or later, a revolutionary breach will come, the consequences of which we cannot possibly foresee.

CHAPTER XI/I.

Up to this time we have been mainly concerned about the difficulties and complications of the Negro question, but no remedy directly for the cure of the malady has been proposed. Now and then suggestions have been offered to meet the demands of certain emergencies, but no general plan as a practical hypothesis has been offered. That something should be done, the tension of conditions in the South abundantly suggests. That something will have to be done sooner or later, all thinking persons readily admit. The perpetual presence of the Negro, the certainty of his remaining in the South, the steady growth of the spirit of worth among the aspiring ones, the struggles of so many thousands to improve their condition, the weakness and criminality of others on the lowest planes, the aversion with which the race is regarded by many whites, which aversion springs chiefly from regarding the Negro from his worst side, the disposition on the part of an irresponsible minority to accord to the Negro only mistreatment and cruelty simply because he is a Negro—all these and other facts are prophetic of future troubles to the country, unless something be

done by the influential whites to relieve the situation.
The task is by no means an easy one. Any course
that might be adopted would doubtless be attended
with difficulty; but it is clear that unless something
be done, the difficulties will thicken in the years of
the future. The strain is not relaxed by time, but
rather made the tauter. Whatever is done will have
to be by the slow process of propitiating public sentiment, which while it may try patience, promises,
after all, the most durable results. No sudden movement will avail anything, it must be the work of
years. But that there lies open a course alike honorable to the white race, and just to the Negro, every
one of equanimity of mind, breadth of observation,
calmness of judgment, and rightness of heart must
believe. Many difficulties previously existing have
been minimized; lessons of vast and deep importance
have been learned alike by the thoughtful of both
races; difficulties which at present exist are now well
defined alike in their nature and scope, and certain
obligations are recognized as imposed, in part, on
both races.

The Negro is not without multitudes of sympa-
thetic friends among the high-minded and enlightened people of the South, who by concert of action,
on the part of even a goodly number, can gradually
succeed in convincing, by a policy of helpfulness,
even many of the most prejudiced that white ignorance and lawlessness are just as bad and dangerous

to the country at large as black ignorance and lawlessness; that the patriotism, integrity, ability, industry, usefulness, thrift, and public spirit on the
part of the Negro, are just as good and are entitled
to as much encouragement and respect and reward
as the capabilities and virtues of the same name
among the whites; that the rights of the white man
are no more sacred than those of the black man,
and that neither white nor black can override the
rights of the other without endangering his own.
These are plain homely principles, which in a season of calmness would seem alike acceptable to all.
A dispassionate recognition of these, followed by a
campaign for their practical expression, in deeds,
would allay multitudes of existing differences, and
rally to the same plane of action the best of both
races. That such cooperation would result in vast
good which, would grow with the years, every one
must see. To be sure, it would encounter opposition, here and there, but the agitation which would
result would be wholesome rather than otherwise,
and show the nature of the opposition to be a policy
against the public good. It would awaken the interest of the able press of the South, the potency of
which would be of vast avail. It would direct the
attention of thousands to the importance of a subject
about which, perhaps, they have thought but little.
But if it should go steadily on, doing its work with
tenacity of purpose, the results would be so gratify-

ing that eventually the races would find their relations and adjustments, and peace would be as prevalent as disorder now is.

Every thoughtful person must recognize the fact that our Southern civilization is largely involved in the treatment which we accord a weaker race which God has placed within our hands as trustees for their elevation and improvement, as well as for His glory. The fact of the sacredness of this charge we cannot shun, even if we would. To its proper consideration we must sooner or later address ourselves as patriots out of a concern for future generations; as philanthropists, in the name of a common humanity, and as Christians, from a bald sense of duty. A duty shunned or a duty delayed is a duty still.

Perhaps we can better arrive at a starting point by the presentation of an accepted principle, and one which has found expression in the practice of years. For many years the different Christian denominations have been sending missionaries to Africa, as well as to other pagan lands. These denominations exercise the same care with respect to the missionaries sent to the Dark Continent that is exercised with respect to those sent elsewhere. They must be men and women of ability and of adaptability to their work; wise and intelligent, and capable of reaching and influencing a people sodden in ignorance and vice, and unacquainted with the sacred principles and advantages offered by the gospel. These missionaries undergo the same investigation as to character and ability to which others sent to other fields of the world are subjected. As Christians, the duty of infusing the gospel into the great black mass of Africans is as readily recognized as is that of reaching and influencing the people of any other race or any other quarter of the globe. Africa is an immense continent on which lives about one-eighth of the population of the globe, and for almost a century, from the first missionary invasion of the Dark Continent, in 1816, by Moffatt, till the present, this land of darkness has claimed our attention. No one asserts among Christians that because these are Africans they are not worthy of the gospel, nor does any one withhold his offerings to African missions on that account.

A missionary from the Southern states, landing on the coast of Africa, must take up his abode among these degraded pagans, and as a wise, consecrated man of God, must sedulously study every possible means of reaching those people. He must necessarily come in contact with them, learn the method of approaching them, and diligently seek a basis of adjustment of himself to existing conditions in order to win them to Christ. Work like this must be unpleasant, much duty is; it must prove oftentimes difficult, as tasks of obligation frequently are; the efforts of the missionary must be attended with much repulsiveness to a refined sense, offending every natural instinct of his cultured character, but he is there on a mission and is constantly impressed by an onerous sense of duty to which all **else** must succumb. What must he do, and what would **we** expect of a missionary under conditions like these? Repulsive and abhorrent as these people might be, sunken in degradation to the lowest limit of morals, and utterly benighted to their destiny, the missionary must stoop to conquer. With keen penetration he must watch for every slight rift in the darkened mass that he may let in the light of life. He cannot scorn or repel them because of their dark skins, their filth and squalor; in spite of these and all else, he must set himself to win them. He cannot by any force of authority compel them to accept the religion which elevates and saves; he must by patience and condescension to their needs win their confidence as the first step toward winning them to God. Nor can he reach them by a denunciation of their vices, or convert them by a display of aversion to them because of their inferior moral status. He cannot produce the slightest impression by leading them to infer that because they are what they are, they are worthy only to be cast out as unworthy. His must be a persuasive mood, one of adjustment to a people who know not God, and to these all else must bend. It doing this the missionary would not be regarded as surrendering his refinement, his ideas of genuine life as he knows it, but as retaining all these while doing the rest. Nor is this an **exagger**ated statement of a situation which has become common in Africa.

Now, instead of that condition, let us suppose another of equal practicalness. Let us suppose that a segment of the population of Africa, numbering several million, is brought to our American shores and assigned to a stipulated portion of our territory. They are pagans still, equally as degraded and sunken as those left in distant Africa. In an event like this, American Christians would be criminally amiss to duty did they not send among these sable savages men and women to win them to righteousness. A colony like the one supposed would be a challenge to American Christians so soon as they touched our borders. That which the missionary does on the Dark Continent would have to be done in this imported population in America. The same studious consideration of the demands of the situation, the same diligent observation of methods to be employed, the same adaptation to prevailing conditions. There would be apparently insuperable barriers to be broken down, numerous and formidable difficulties to be overcome, and discouragement on discouragement to be constantly met; but duty would meet all these with a courageous front, and the missionary among these imported pagans would press on in his work. Whether there were immediate visible signs of encouragement or not, he would persist in his endeavors, for to surrender would be to deny the efficacy of the gospel to dissolve all moral difficulty.

But in the presence of a concrete condition we are left neither to supposition nor theory. Here are

the Africans at our doors. Here they are by millions. How they came to be here is well known.
While they have been the recipients of certain advantages, it is well known what they have undergone.
Their history in America has been one of long en-
slavement, of irksome servitude, and of restricted
privilege. Of the result of these the white race has
been the abundant recipient. Without any direct in-
strumentality of their own, the Negro in America
has been brought into peculiar relations with the
white race, and into such relations as impose onerous
obligations on the stronger people. These obligations spring from several grounds, among which
is that of gratitude for that which the Negro has
done for the enrichment of the country, and the elevation of the stronger race by the means afforded
by the Negro for such elevation. Independent of
this, and even had it not occurred, would be the
ground of philanthropy, because of the condition of
the race. In addition, still, would be the demand
of humanity because of the racial relations. Then,
there is the ground of chivalry because of the relation of the stronger to the weaker, and last of all
would be the ground of Christianity because of the
obligation everywhere imposed on that system to
raise the fallen.

By these conditions and obligations are we today
confronted. They are inexorable principles to
which we dare not close our ears and eyes. Nor
are they to be dismissed by subtlety of reas-

oning or by the makeshift of excuse. We can no
more reason them out of existence than we can
shovel darkness out of an unlighted room. This
duty, these facts, these principles, we must meet as
men and as Christians. To deny them does not remove the obligation. The white race is the creator
of the present situation, is responsible for it as the
original importers of the black man to America, and
on him is imposed the duty of relieving the situation.

However, this burden is greatly relieved by many
encouraging conditions. In dealing with the Negro
as he is, he deals not with a pagan. He does not
have to study his approaches to the heart and mind
of the Negro. He knows him at his best, at his
worst. Conditions are well defined. He understands his weakness as he does his strength. He
understands the Negro's habits and the means of
reaching and of influencing him. The gateways to
his nature lie open. Many thousands of Negroes are
Christians. Other thousands of them have climbed
high up the ladder of our splendid American civilization. Multitudes of them are intelligent, thrifty,
progressive, wide-awake in the production of prosperity, laborious, useful in thousands of ways, while
other multitudes of them need just the aid and encouragement which the whites only can give. If
duty respecting this people is inexorable, it is stimulated by many elements of encouragement. In any
effort to aid and to elevate, the two higher classes
would prove invaluable allies in assisting in the ele-

vation of the lower elements of the race to a higher plane of life. Was ever Christianity confronted by an obligation plainer? Was ever a vaster field opened to philanthropy? Was ever Christian duty more suggestive and urgent?

There is not the smallest doubt, even for a moment, on the part of those who know the Negro, that the two higher classes of blacks would respond most readily to any effort made to elevate the Negro race. They would account it a privilege to make any possible sacrifice for the attainment of this end. The mere fact that the white race would enter on a campaign like this would rally every worthy Negro to its support. Negroes are a responsive people, and in the light of experience of late years, they would be doubly so now. This fact strengthens the obligation to assist them to better things in life. Should a policy like this be entered on what would be the result? It would allay differences which now operate to the detriment of both races by the estrangement occasioned and the bitterness engendered; it would weld into cooperation the best forces of both races, which in itself would constitute a condition of confidence and harmony which does not now exist, and this without the impairment of the segregation of the races, which is much desired on the part of the better blacks as it is by the better whites; while the boundaries of cooperative effort would touch at many points, it would not mean racial fusion; it would prove mutually beneficial to both races, by lifting the colored race up to a plane of merit, while it would make the white man better for the effort thus made; it would level the existing barriers in the highway of prosperity, dismiss the apprehensions which haunt the future, and illustrate anew the prowess of the Anglo-Saxon in grappling with a difficult situation and in conquering it. All this is possible, and while it would require years in order to reach a gratifying consummation, it can be accomplished. The identity of interest would come to be recognized, and the Negro would prove to be the best friend the white man has. Among all the colored races he is today the white man's best friend.

A policy like this would be in thorough accord with the spirit of the times. We are living in a peculiar period. It is a juncture of eras. It is a period of transition from the old to the new. Old habitudes of thought, old customs, old systems, all the beaten paths of policy and of custom are being abandoned for a sphere that is new. It is a breaking-up period. The crash of old orders is heard throughout the world, and a new system is being ushered in. In all this, the Anglo-Saxon is leading. His ideas of right and of liberty are transforming the world. Wherever he plants his flag, prosperity blooms and fruits. The world is in the throes of a tremendous upheaval. While views are shifting and sentiments are changing, principles which never change are assuming new phases. Back of all this are the dynamic principles which the Nazarene came to ex-

pound to the nations and generations of men.
Christianity exalts, and as the dynamic force of the
ages, it has raised man to a higher level by successive
revolution. It has brought us face to face with an
opportunity which no nation has hitherto enjoyed—
that of elevating a race and of making it capable
of becoming a mighty factor in a land to which that
race is as loyal as the most patriotic of the Anglo-
Saxon. In a period like this, when human liberty
and rights are uppermost in the minds of men everywhere, the opportunity is afforded of according to
the imported African the merits of his just deserts.
The Negro is human, he is a man, and as such we
must deal with him. Preconceived notions and opinions, prejudices previously formed, and all else, must
yield to the demand of duty—duty between man and
man.

We have the situation before us. What is our
duty to the Negro race? What can be done? What
should be done? The Negro craves not pity, he
pleads not helplessness—all that he asks is that which
is due him as a man. That he should do this is to
his credit, and instead of exciting opposition should
command our respect the more. He asks that the
circumscriptions which have so long operated to the
cramp of his powers be removed that he may be able
to stand on his feet and vindicate his claim to genuine manhood. He desires not to be fondled and
cajoled, but that he be unfettered to join in the rough
encounters of the world. He insists not that the

stronger race give him a fish, but only a hook. Not till the Negro proves utterly unworthy, not till he becomes a loathesome burden too heavy to be borne, should we talk of his repudiation. Certainly not while he strikes out with the boldness with which he has done to help to overcome the difficulties which encumber his people, should he have other than words of cheer and inspiration, and the moral support of his brother in white. While the Negro has never been without his friends, both South and North, the question is, Why should not all alike be his friends? It is well known that the blunders of the reconstruction period were not his, but those of men who were actuated by self-aggrandizement. Of this not a few of them learned after it was too late.* Betrayed into this condition, he should not be held entirely responsible, and certainly this should not be charged against him now. If some are criminals, they deserve to be dealt with as common criminals, with all that belongs to such. Even

*In the History of the Last Quarter Century, by E. Benjamin Andrews, he furnishes the following extract from a letter written by the colored senator from Mississippi, Hon. Hiram R. Revels, to President Grant, in the early '70s, which illustrates the conditions in the South at that time. The extract is as follows:

"Since reconstruction the masses of people have been, as it were, enslaved in mind by unprincipled adventurers. A great portion of them have learned that they were being used as mere tools, and determined by casting their ballots against these unprincipled adventurers to overthrow them. The bitterness and hate created by the late civil strife (local troubles in Mississippi) have, in my opinion, been obliterated in this State, except, perhaps in some localities, and would have long since been effaced were it not for some unprin-

criminals have rights in a democracy. Nor should the entire race have laid at its door the crimes of the few. *I*s there nothing worthy of a multitudinous race that can be done by the stronger race of Anglo-Saxons?

Since near the close of the seventeenth century, which signally marks a period when the humanitarian idea began to take hold on men, and which found expression in various organizations and through the medium of literature at a later time, there have sprung up movements for the amelioration of the human family. One of the first organizations which sprang from this spirit was one which was called the Society for Promoting Christian Knowledge, and later The Society for the Propagation of the Gospel in Foreign Parts. Crude and cumbersome as these original humanitarian organizations were, they wrought a mighty work for good, and opened the way for the great missionary organizations throughout the world.

Could there be begun in these American states a society for the promotion of the good of the Negro, which could be so directed as to reach him at every

cipled men who would keep alive the bitterness of the past and inculcate a hatred between the races in order that they may aggrandize themselves by office and its emoluments to control my people, the effect of which is to degrade them. If the State administration had advanced patriotic measures, appointed only honest and competent men to office, and sought to restore confidence between the races, bloodshed would have been unknown, peace would have prevailed, Federal inteference been unthought of, and harmony, friendship, and mutual confidence would have taken the place of the bayonet."

point of his life, socially, industrially, commercially, educationally, benevolently, and morally, what a mighty transformation might be wrought in these American states! Much has been done for the Negro's education, and all hail to the philanthropists who have rendered such aid, yet it has been of a fractional sort, and by piecemeal, each working in its own way. Could there be such a combination of effort as would resolve all others into unity and under separate divisions or departments, directed from a common center, a few years would witness a tremendous change in the country. A movement like this would acquaint the world with the growing worth of the Negro, and his merits would be as well known as his crimes and short-comings now are. This would require management and direction of a colossal character, but of no greater proportions than are some of the mammoth commercial organizations now existing. It would mark a new era in the progress of Anglo-Saxonism, and of the refluent consequences on the fatherland of the Negro, none could tell. More than anything else, it would lead to the Christianization of Africa, as well as other regions where the habitats of the Negro are over the habitable globe. It would infuse fresh life into the Negro population of the American states, and prove not alone a blessing to the African-American, but would be far-reaching in its effects over the world.

It would set an educative example to other peoples of the world, and the moral influence would be unspeakable. Christianity has an opportunity in the present status of the Negro race in America such as it has rarely enjoyed since its introduction to the world. The Negro can survive in regions in which the white man cannot. He could take with him to Africa and other regions where the Negro lives, a knowledge of the civilization of which he has been made a beneficiary in America, and along with this would be the dispensation of the gospel. In the midst of the great world movements of the present, none would eclipse a movement like this.

CHAPTER XIV.

It is admitted that if the Negro had remained a leaden mass, cold, inflexible, inanimate, after his emergence from slavery, there would now be but slight hope and little encouragement to assist him to reach higher levels in life. But this is far from being true. While some are indolent and even worthless, hundreds of thousands have met the difficulties which have beset them, at every step, and with a grim determination worthy of any race, have made remarkable progress. It is easy to decry an entire race because of the worthlessness of the few, but sheer justice demands that honor be accorded to whom it is due.

In urging the claims of the Negro race on the Christian philanthropy of the American states, in the chapter immediately preceding, there were presented supposed cases in missionary endeavor both with respect to work among the pagans on the Dark Continent and those who might have been landed on our own shores. Instead of encountering the corrupt paganism in Africa, suppose the missionary should find that a majority of the people could read and write, and that among them were orators, educators, editors, ministers of the gospel, lawyers, druggists, artisans, skilled mechanics, and **repre-**sentatives of the various crafts of civilization. Suppose, too, he should find millions of Christians with thousands of houses of worship, devoted to the propagation of the true religion, would he not hail a condition like this with joy? Would this not be true concerning any people among whom missionary endeavor was made?

This is true concerning the Negro in America. In view of these facts, it may be said that if any people have ever won the consideration of a Christian nation, the American Negro has, because of his efforts under disadvantages the greatest, and because of the success which he has been enabled to achieve. Lying back of present conditions, it should not be lost sight of that the Negro is at least worthy of our gratitude because of his centuries of unrewarded toil, but especially since his freedom, has the Negro proved his worth by his struggles to ascend to the highest attainment possible, and that, too, in the face of giant difficulties which he has mastered, and mastered in spite of every possible handicap. A situation like this affords a broad basis of encouragement and hopefulness.

That a movement similar to the one already named in behalf of the entire race of Negroes would elicit fresh energy on the part of the race in its own behalf, and, in turn, stimulate it to newer exertion, seems certain from our knowledge of the Negro. Instead of creating undue assertion on the part of the Negro, as some are disposed to think, it would beget an humble gratitude, and immensely relax the strained relations between the two races, white and black. By the Negro it would be hailed as an omen of better things, and as an advent of conditions that would restore confidence and a spirit of restfulness. In view of a prospect like this, there is the amplest encouragement for action. Unless there be a desire for a continuation of racial tension and a perpetuation of conditions that will be productive of race disharmony, some movement for the relief of the present situation will have to be inaugurated which will guarantee protection to the Negro, and afford such aid as will enable him to become of the greatest possible advantage to himself and to the country at large. Rancor and prejudice are the teeth of dragons the harvests of which will produce fresher and graver problems for other generations to solve. To adopt a course which will gradually propitiate public sentiment is the policy wisdom would now recommend, prudence suggest, and sanity dictate. Present troubles will not be relieved by delay, but fostered the rather, and in dispassionate conduct, in the creation of mutual confidence, lies our only hope. We may enact drastic legislation for the control of the Negro, but what then? That only means the cultivation of a new crop of criminals, who in a desperate and hardened condition are turned loose anew on society, to foster fresh crimes and perpetrate new deeds of wrong. What would be the consequence

of that condition? The lawless Negro invites counter lawlessness on the part of the white man, and
demoralization, in divers forms, becomes a routine in
every Southern community.

Looking further into the sources of encouragement, we find certain other auguries of inspiration.
In an impoverished condition, the Negro emerged,
in 1865, from slavery, and unmurmuringly faced the
future. His has been a steadily and laboriously upward climb. While some other races would have
disintegrated under the stress and strain, the Negro
has continued to multiply. Within fifteen years after
the advent of freedom, the Negroes had increased
from 4,550,000 to 6,580,793, and by the end of the
nineteenth century, or by 1900, the increase was 34.2
per cent, or 8,833,944. The next census will reveal
that the Negro race has gone to 10,000,000, or about
one-eighth of the population of the country. Negroes
have thrived and increased in spite of the innumerable disadvantages encountered. The Negro race
is virile, prolific, and flexible, and responds in adjustment to all conditions, but all the while it multiplies.

What progress has the race made meanwhile?
Within twenty-five years after emancipation this
penniless population of ignorant blacks, though
meeting opposition at every step of the way, had
reached that stage of progress that 372,414 had come
to own homes of their own, and 4,000,000 of them
were engaged in profitable vocations, 34 per cent of

whom were agricultural laborers, farmers and overseers. Among these were those of such exceptional ability and management, that, beginning as share tenants, they became cash tenants, then partly owners of property, and finally complete owners. The merit of such progress becomes more conspicuous when we bear in mind that thirty-five years before, they were ignorant and poverty-stricken, and in the struggle to accumulate, they had met with the mightiest of disadvantages.

According to the census of 1900, or thirty-five years after the dawn of freedom, the Negroes had acquired in the South Central States 95,624 farms, while the tenants of land numbered 348,805, or 21.5 per cent of all the farms within that group of states. Within the same period of thirty-five years, the Negroes in the South Atlantic States had acquired 287,933 farms, of which number 70.4 were tenants, and 29.6 were owners outright. Yet three and a half decades before not one of these in either of the group of states named, owned an inch of land or a dollar in money. It is a remarkable fact that the growth of land owners among the Negroes, within the same period of years, was three-fourths as rapid as the relative number of owners among the whites. The total value of Negro farm property in the group already named amounted to $300,000,000, and including improvements, it amounted to $350,000,000, to which when the valuation of implements and live stock are added approximate in value $500,000,000.

Ten years ago, or when the last national census was taken, there were in Virginia 26,566 Negro land owners; in Mississippi, 21,973; in Texas, 20,139; in South Carolina, 18,970; in North Carolina, 17,520; in Alabama, 14,110; in Arkansas, 11,941; in Georgia, 11,375; in Tennessee, 9,426; in Louisiana 9,371; in Florida, 6,552; in Kentucky, 5,402; in Maryland, 2,262; in West Virginia, 534; in Delaware, 332, and in the District of Columbia, 5.

Nor does this list include real estate owned in the towns and cities, in which there are thousands of establishments of business, including stores, offices, banks, office buildings, residences for rent, hotels, churches, and much else. This represents the property showing of the Negro ten years ago, and his holdings have rapidly increased since that time. If so much was done during the first generation following the year of emancipation, when the Negro was deficient in intelligence, wisdom, experience, and forethought, what may we reasonably expect of him within the next generation?

Widely scattered through the states of the South, this progress has gone quietly on, and so quietly, that to many it was an occasion of surprise when the census reports were published. While unaware of these facts, the public was duly informed of the faults and crimes of the worst class of Negroes, as these expressions of lawlessness were exploited in the public prints of the country. This suggests the fact that if the merits of the worthy Negroes were as well known as the crimes of the few, and they the worst, the sentiment of the public concerning the colored race would be vastly different. It is an unfortunate fact that one of the principal assets of the race question is that of the mutual ignorance of both races concerning one another. The gravest of questions before the American public is the one about which least is known.

The educational strides made by the Negro are as astonishing as are those made in material progress. Among the commendable aspirations of the Negro is that of the acquisition of an education. The sacrifices made by Negro parents for the education of their children are alike pathetic and praiseworthy. In consequence of this, illiteracy among Negroes has annually declined. In 1880, of the Negro population above ten years of age, 70 per cent was illiterate. By the end of the next decade, or in 1890, this illiteracy had been reduced to 57.1 per cent, and by the close of the century it was re duced to 44.5 per cent. During the last ten years of the nineteenth century, there was an increase of the Negro population of 1,087,000 in the school age of ten years and over; yet, despite this increase, there was a decrease of illiteracy of 190,000. This tells the story of pinched livelihoods, untold sacrifice, frugality, struggle and aspiration. These facts lie within the realm of unwritten history, but the aggregation of dry figures means much of which the world can never know. If so much has been done in the face of discouragement by the Negro, what might have been accomplished had the conditions been the opposite?

From some to whom these facts are known, have come the suggested apprehension of that which is popularly known as Negro supremacy. Such a suggestion is unworthy the Caucasian. To quote the language of another Southerner: "The old cry that 'white supremacy' may be imperilled is a travesty of Anglo-Saxon chivalry. With every executive, judicial, and legislative office of the state in the hands of the white people, and with suffrage qualifications that have practically eliminated the Negro from political affairs, the old slogan is the emptiest cant.

"This is no question for small politicians, but for broad, patriotic statesmen. It is not one for nonresident theorists, but for practical publicists; not one for academic sentimentalists, but one for clear-visioned humanitarians. On a subject of such vital concern to state and nation, passionate declamation and partisan denunciation are to be deplored. Oh, that some patriot may arise, with the prescience of a statesman and the vision of a prophet and the soul of an apostle, who will point out the path of a national duty, and guide our people to a wise and heaven-approved solution of this mighty problem."*

*From an address delivered by Bishop Charles B. Galloway, of the M. E. Church, South, on the occasion of the Seventh Annual Conference for Education in the South, Birmingham, Ala., April 26, 1904.

Nothing can be effected by constant ill speaking against the Negro, and by an underestimate of his worth. If we are ever to begin the solution of the Negro question it must start by shifting prejudice to a basis of recognized obligation of duty to him as a man, and of right and justice to him in the spheres in which he moves. To speak of expediency as a course to be pursued is to ignore these fundamental ethical grounds, unless, indeed, we bear in mind that principle is the path of highest expediency. When ten million Ethiopians in these American states stretch forth their hands to the Christians of America, what reply will they make? When they ask for aid will we reply with a taunt or a blow? When they endeavor to rise in the scale of being, will we seek to repel them? When they aspire to worth, shall we close to them the door of opportunity? When by sacrifice and painful effort, in the face of fierce competition, they qualify themselves for efficient service, shall they be regarded as rivals, and be driven out of legitimate pursuits?

It will be remembered that in the early part of the year 1909, there was a strike of remonstrance on the part of the white engineers on the Georgia Railroad because the management of that corporation was seeking to "place them on the same equality with the Negro." The demand was extended so as to embrace the idea that the Negro firemen be eliminated and stipulated for other minor concessions. Not a little violence of divers sorts followed, and for weeks, the entire country was engrossed with the affair. That this should have occurred in Georgia, which had so long been considered one of the most conservative states of the South, and that it should have come so soon after the notorious outbreak in the city of Atlanta, lent increased interest to the matter. As a result of the strike, violence was visited on not a few colored men, the trains were stopped, the mails ceased, general business was interfered with, provisions became scarce along the road, and general disorder prevailed.

After weeks of disturbance, it was agreed to submit the question in dispute, for settlement, to a board of arbitration composed of Chancellor David C. Barrow, of the University of Georgia; Hon. Hilary A. Herbert, secretary of the navy under Cleveland, and Hon. T. W. Hardwick, congressman from Augusta, who represented the firemen. The decision of the board was just and equitable, it being that the railroad shall be allowed to employ Negro firemen whenever the same are qualified to render efficient service, and that the wages of the Negroes thus employed shall be the same as that of the whites for the same character of service. The proceedings of the board thus appointed were watched with keen interest throughout, and when the final decision was announced, the expressions which came from the press of the country showed not alone the interest felt in the matter, but voiced a sentiment that was gratifying, and disclosed the latent thought of the public concerning the Negro, South, as well as North. Some of those expressions are given here to show the sentiment concerning the Negro, not only, but within these expressions of opinion are indications of conditions which if marshalled and organized would settle many elements in the much-vexed race question. The extracts are furnished from some of the representative papers of the South as well as of the North.

The Columbia (S. C.) *State* commended the action of the board, and then proceeded to say: "To have decided against the right of the Negro firemen to make a living, to have yielded to the unreasonable and selfish and prejudiced demands of the white firemen of the Georgia Railroad, to have yielded the crucial point of justice and right, would have been nothing less than a calamity, not only to Georgia but to the South."

From another point of view is the question considered by the Chattanooga (Tenn.) *Times,* which insisted that the decision "means that in view of the most influential leaders among Southern men, the Negro shall have a right to earn a living in the South in any sphere of manual or technical labor for which he may be fit."

The Augusta (Ga.) *Chronicle,* which was on the scene of the disturbance, takes a more comprehensive view of the situation. *It* said: "Inasmuch as the Negro constitutes the bulk of the South's laboring population, to take away from him the right to labor—'side by side with the white man'—when necessary, would place the heaviest possible handicap upon the South itself; for it would not only have a surplus of idle Negroes to contend with, but a scarcity of labor in all industrial pursuits."

Other southern papers were equally as pronounced, but these are furnished as fair samples of Southern sentiment regarding the Negroes in this unnatural and unjustified revolt.

Turning now to the North, quotations are made from some of the leading journals of that quarter. The New York *Evening Post* pronounced the decision of the arbitrators "a gratifying triumph of common sense and common honesty." While the Boston *Transcript* regarded the settlement with a goodly degree of doubt and called the decision a "two-edged sword," it manifested an interest which showed that a regard for the Negro and his welfare retains a firm hold on the public mind. It said: "Outwardly this appears like a splendid exhibition of fair play between the two races, but practically whenever an employer is compelled by statute, or by agreement with labor-unions, or by public sentiment to equalize wages in disregard of economic law, the result is usually that he takes the class which could only be had at the higher figure."

The New York *World* took the view that "in the long run it is the white labor of the South that will profit most from the Negro's economic equality," and then proceeds to say "when such equality is established, white labor has nothing to fear from Negro competition. The superior intelligence of the white man and his greater productive capacity are a continuing insurance against his displacement. In the higher ranks of artisans and mechanics only a relatively small number of Negroes will attain the white standard, but the door of hope will be closed to no man.

"But if the Negro is to be discriminated against on a wage basis, merely because he is a Negro, an irrepressible industrial conflict is created in which white labor is bound to lose. The cheaper labor will drive the higher-priced labor out of employment, just as slave labor brought the poor whites to shiftlessness and degradation.

"Equal pay for equal work, for white and black alike, is the only road to industrial security for the white labor of the South. On this issue the Negro's cause is the white man's cause."

The New York *Tribune* took up the matter in a more judicial spirit and expressed the thought "that it is by no means certain the decision will eliminate the Negro" and continued by saying: "Even at the same wages employers may prefer to employ a certain proportion of Negroes, because the Negro is not unionized, and the prospect of labor troubles will be lessened. Moreover, white labor is not abundant in the South, and the Negro may find his opportunity for that reason. *It* is interesting to see the first appearance in the South of this favorite device of the labor-unions to crowd out cheaper labor. With regard to the labor of women in the North the unions have adopted the same equal pay attitude; in unionized trades women must receive the same wages as men. No doubt we shall hear more of the same doctrine in the South. Its effect if generally put in force would be problematical there. In some trades it might mean preference for the cheaper Negro labor and the elimination of the whites. That would be impossible on the railroads, however, since white firemen must be retained in order to recruit engineers from their ranks."

While these expressions were generally favorable, there were not wanting some papers which represent a lesser aspect of thought which expressed unfavorable comment on the decision reached by the board of arbitrators. But this was to be expected, as the source represented that which was unfavorable to the Negro. The fact that this emergency was possible in the states of the South, shows the necessity of the timely interposition of just such a force as was here called into requisition, the character of which will be needed again as future exigencies will arise. But the fact that the Negro was vindicated on the basis of merit alone, is a favorable augury. As he increases in importance and industrial value, he will need more and more the interposition of the better class of whites.

One of the difficulties respecting the relations of the two races is that the large worthy class of Negroes come but rarely into contact with the better elements of the white population of the South. Their pursuits and vocations lie apart in distinct spheres of action, and but little is known of that which each is doing. Events already named severed them, and the disposition to recount only the misdeeds of the unworthy Negroes has built up a partition between the two races. Induced into coöperation with the best whites, this higher and worthier class of Negroes are in position to render effectual aid in relieving the situation of much of its stress. Any specific movement looking in that direction on the part of the philanthropic white men would be hailed as a happy augury by this class of Negroes, who are in position to assist as no other agency can. It would seem that nothing short of a general popular movement which would bring into exercise the best of both races, will relieve the situation in the South, and the importance of a movement like this would suggest that it not be delayed.

The worth which the Negro has established in the South makes it important that some action be taken in his behalf. He is not without thousands of friends among the better people of the South, but the sentiment is dissipated and unorganized. The time must come sooner or later when the matter must claim the attention of the best people of the

country in a more general and generous way than it
has yet done.*

*In The World's Work for October, 1909, in a brief sketch
given of Robert S. Lovett, the successor to Mr. Harriman,
appears the following under the head of "Mr. Harriman's
Chief of Staff":

"One day last summer Judge Lovett received from a com-
mittee of prominent citizens of Houston, Texas, a long letter
asking that he make it his business to see that white men be
given the first chance to fill vacancies in the switching yards
at Houston caused by the dropping of Negroes. In his reply
he took up and demolished the 'reasons' set forth by the
citizens. The concluding paragraphs of the letter are worth
quoting as an illustration of the manner of the man's mind
in dealing with public questions:

"'Another reason given in the petition from the citizens
of Houston is, "We believe that positions paying the wages
these positions do should be in the hands of white men."
This simply means that Negroes shall not be allowed to do
work that pays good wages whenever there are white men
who want the job. Where is the line to be drawn upon the
rate of wages and the kind of labor the Negro shall be allowed? If this company must not employ them as switchmen,
may they be employed as section men, porters, sawmill hands,
bricklayers, teamsters, warehouse laborers, barbers, gardeners,
farmers, or in any of the other pursuits in which they must
labor to live? It would be just as right and reasonable to
replace the Negro in any of these occupations with white men,
simply because the latter want the job, as to replace the Negro
switchmen of this company, who are doing their work well,
with white men, merely because they want the positions.

"'If the policy thus urged upon this company is to be the
policy of the South toward the Negro; if he is to be allowed
to do only such labor as no white man will do, and receive
only such wages as no white man wants, what is to become
of the Negroes? How are they to live? Food and clothes
they must have. If not by labor how are they to get the
necessaries of life? Hunger must and will be satisfied—
prisons and chain-gangs notwithstanding.

"'After most careful and respectful considerations, none
of the reasons suggested and none I have been able to think
of justifies me to committing this company in any way to a
policy fraught with such far-reaching consequences and so
much opposed to my own sense of justice to faithful
servants.'"

Judge Lovett is a Southern man, having been born and
reared in Texas.

CHAPTER XV.

It is interesting to compare the predictions made by many, in the outset of Negro freedom in the South, when the Negro was penniless and friendless, and was turned loose with a liberty which was a positive embarrassment to him, with the theories which came to prevail after he began to realize the force of the meaning of his liberation, and entered on a course of steady advancement in intellectual improvement and material development. At first, he was deemed incapable of advancement, and the prediction was made that he would become an incubus and a burden to society because of his incapacity. It was honestly believed by not a few that he would be unable to cope with existing conditions in the scrambles of life, and that his drift would be toward paganism. In the initial stages of freedom his efforts were crude and bungling, and were a source of much merriment. But as he has pursued his torturous way, manifesting first of all an avidity for learning in the schools, and as he has turned to practical account the slight advantages within his reach, and has gradually gained a footing in life, prospering as he has gone, opinions have undergone a radical change, and favorable sentiment is now turning toward him. The anomalous position and condition of the race exposed it to the curious gaze of the public, as every one was anxious to see what it would be able to make of its novel freedom. As the race has pursued its way, procuring what was afforded by the educational facilities placed at its disposal, building homes, building houses of worship, and manning them with a ministry trained in the schools, bought lands and tilled it with profit to itself and to the state, established schools of its own, and conducted them by the most approved means of modern instruction, sending, meanwhile, its representatives into the different professions, founded banks and established stores, many of which are patronized by the whites, developed leaders of wisdom and of power, who are slowly getting a grip on the race for its improvement, and as orators, authors, editors, educators, surgeons, bankers, managers, hotel keepers, planters and others have been developed, original predictions of failure have been changed into theories of apprehension, lest the race attain to an importance which may not only bring it into acute competition with the Caucasian race, but occasion such conditions as will result in race conflict.

Not a few have been the efforts made by noisy lecturers, and prejudiced authors of a certain type of literature, to have it appear that the Negro is rising to such prominence as to imperil even "white supremacy." Had the original conceptions been realized respecting the Negro, he would have been despised, but now that the opposite is true, he is, by a given class, envied and feared. Various have been the apprehensions expressed in the event of certain contingencies concerning the progress of the Negro, but in every instance, these have proved groundless with the arrival of the facts. It has been found that these apprehensions have been more the results of the imagination than those of realization. As the gateways one by one have opened to the Negro, he has quietly entered them, efficiently done his work, and it has been found that the world has a place for the Negro, and when he has reached it, he has fitted himself into it as do all other men. The result of this has generally been an appreciation of his adaptability and readiness to respond to conditions, and has served to evoke due meed of praise. The Negro has not been slow to acquire much wisdom and to learn many important lessons in the ups and downs of his career, among which is that when they bring to an assumed undertaking ability to accomplish, there has not been withheld the proper accord of merit. As a result of this steady condition, all fears have vanished and all theories have dissolved where Negroes have brought to tasks in life ability to accomplish that to which they have set their hands. One instance will serve to illustrate others. An intelligent and prudent young colored man, a graduate from one of the colored schools of the South, went to a town in one of the South Atlantic states, procured a piece of land and began the erection of a school building for the purpose of teaching the young Negroes of that region the methods of agricultural industry. He was quietly waited on by a body of white citizens, who after learning of his purpose, informed him that they were opposed to his project, as it would bode no good to the town, nor to the Negroes of that region, and advised him that he must desist from further procedure. He assured them that no such conditions as those which they apprehended would result, and gave assurance that if he be allowed to proceed with his enterprise, they would have no occasion to regret the reversal of their decision. His plea was so assuring and submissive withal, that they agreed to hold their objections in abeyance and await the test. The school building was completed and duly opened, was continued with increased usefulness from year to year, with such wholesome results on the Negro population of that region, and with so much financial profit to the town, that every worthy white citizen would now protect it against any attempted assault or even against adverse criticism.

It is not from the worthy class of blacks that troubles come in the South. Where they make themselves worthy and indispensable, where they can do things better and for less money than can others, they are sought. Such as these never fail to make for themselves positions of respectability which is duly accorded. In another Southern town a well-to-do Negro casually passed two white men on the street. The Negro is a thrifty business man, owning several houses for rent and a good plantation, besides a bank account of which any ordinary citizen might feel proud. As he was passed, one of the whites turned to the other and said, "It is all I can do to keep from calling that nigger, Mister." The incident, though trifling, is not without abundance of suggestion.

While the apprehension has materially lessened because it has so often been eclipsed by concrete fact, yet it still lurks in many minds that the better equipment of the Negro intellectually would prove an injury to himself and to society at large; but when the effort is made to summon the facts in proof of this, they are usually found wanting. The Negro takes the place which the world provides for him. His efficiency readily adapts him to his sphere. With him it is as true as it is of all others, life is what he makes it. In no community in the South do people suffer in consequence of Negroes who know something and are prepared to do something. The truth is that such are sought, and will continue to be. Not the slightest apprehension is created by the class of well-to-do Negroes of the South. It is a noteworthy fact that no graduate from either Hampton or Tuskegee has ever been accused of even the slightest impropriety of conduct toward ladies. It is equally to the credit of these schools and to the work which they are doing for the colored race, that none of their graduates have been sentenced to the penitentiary. *If* intelligence and general equipment are dangerous weapons in the hands of the Negro, the fact would long ago have been developed by at least one of these products from these schools. Nor is it true that this class of colored people are unduly assertive and mandatory of special rights and favors. All observation proves that they are usually the quietest of the Negro population, and the most submissive to wrongs imposed. The culture acquired so disposes them. That there may be exceptions of undue assumption, is not denied. It would be most marvelous if this were not so. But these slight exceptions, if they be, do not prove the rule, as every well-informed person in the South knows. True, an exception respecting the Negro usually goes further than when commonly applied, as to the conduct of one to the many, yet the absence of the exceptions means much.

It is ordinarily the case that wherever one is able, by dint of effort and economy, to buy and till land, to found and maintain a home, and to become a producer of marketable commodities in a community, he is by virtue of these facts, a much better man and citizen. Observation teaches that efficiency and literacy promote thrift, self-respect, interest in the general welfare of the community, and strength of character, whether these pertain to the white, red, black or saffron races of men. To elevate men so that they can observe and think for themselves, and act for themselves, is infinitely better than to repress them by sheer force and control them by the sternness of law. As President Booker T. Washington pithily puts it, "One man cannot hold another down in the ditch without remaining down there himself."

Touching the race question, it should always be borne in mind that not only are there two races involved but two sides of an issue, as well. Whatever benefits the Negro will benefit the white man; and contrariwise, whatever works to the detriment of the one, by a law inseparable from the very condition of things, works to the detriment of the other. The relation of the two races make this an inexorable principle. The races must stand or fall together. If drastic measures are employed to the exclusion of justice and mercy, the reaction is one of hardness and the general impairment of character on the part of the inflicter. In order to repress the Negro we must necessarily depress the standard of our own manhood. We may gratify revenge by undue advantage taken, but such gratification reacts in a tendency toward savagery, with the certainty of an inexorable law. No one can escape the consequences to character of cherished sentiments and overt action. To cheer, aid, inspire and relieve broadens one, while another is helped.

> "He is dead whose hand is not opened wide
> To help the need of a human brother;
> He doubles the length of his life-long ride
> Who of his fortune gives to another;

And a thousand million lives are his
Who carries the world in his sympathies.
    To deny
    Is to die."

As has already been pointed out, from the dire predictions of years ago of the incapacity of the Negro, there has come to pass, in these later times, an apprehension of the industrial rivalry of the Negro. *I*t is certainly not creditable to the Anglo-Saxon, with centuries of culture and advantage behind him, and with the most splendid civilization the world has ever known at his ready command, to lisp a syllable of apprehension concerning the rivalry of the Negro in any particular. *I*t is difficult to determine which is more involved in such an apprehension, the conscious inferiority of the Caucasian or a tremendous compliment to the lately-enslaved Negro. The Anglo-Saxon who ventures to utter such apprehension does his race great discredit. In the multiplicity of industrial opportunities afforded, and in the vast, untouched domain of that which is yet to be done, it sounds like the refinement of sarcasm to express the slightest fear in behalf of the growing efficiency of the Negro. It is not too much to say that if the white man, with all his boundless advantages, is to be surpassed by the Negro, with his numerous handicaps, then he is worthy of being excelled. So far from fearing the Negro, there is not an Anglo-Saxon who should not from his exalted advantage be ready to inspire every worthy Negro to do his best in personal improvement and for the public good.

But one of the chiefest of the concerns in the minds of some in the states of the South, is that of the assertion of the Negro, in his ambition to attain to equality in social life. Possibly no apprehension is more far-fetched and strained than this one. Certainly none is more groundless, yet it has been a popular bugaboo for almost a generation. For years it has been a favorite slogan of the stump in the lips of the paltry demagogue. It has furnished to the cheap lecturer on the platform not a little of prejudicial material, and to a certain class of mercenary authors of sensational novels, it has been an occasion of bonanzas. It disturbs not the class of people whose width of information and of observation justifies no such apprehension. They see no occasion of such fear. Nor is there occasioned with this class other than ridicule because of the entertainment of a fear like this.

Certainly there has been nothing on the part of the Negro to justify it. If such assertion should be made it would come first from the class of intelligent and progressive blacks. We should look naturally first in that direction for such a demonstration. Has it been made? Are they not really the best-behaved and the least demonstrative of the Negro people? In this respect they have occasioned no more trouble than they have in any other. They

are orderly and uniformly polite and more concess-
ive than any others. *In* justice to the educated
Negro and to his credit, let this testimony be borne.

Perhaps the apprehension is due chiefly to certain
expressions of protest on the part of Negroes, as
occasionally but seldom made, because of the gross
injustice experienced by them on the common carriers. They have not resisted the separation of the
races into "jimcrow" compartments, but they have
protested against the inferiority of the accommoda-
tions sometimes, yea, oftentimes afforded, and the
unjust discrimination of certain corporations by
declining to provide equal facilities of comfort for
a uniform rate of travel. Alike by most of the
Southern states and cities there has been adopted
the method of separate apartments, on the common
carriers, for the two races, with the theoretical provision of uniform facilities for uniform rates. Yet
it is a fact commonly known, that while the fares
have been uniform, the facilities of comfort have
not been. At times, Negroes have protested against
this discrimination, and justly. So far from this expression on the part of the Negro exciting apprehension and opposition, lest it savor of demands of
social equality, it should excite our appreciation of
the Negro. Because he does thus insist on fair
treatment at the hands of the corporations, we
should the more respect him. He has a clear right
for that for which he has paid, and a chivalrous
public sentiment should interpose to see to it that

greedy corporations be not allowed to take advantage of the Negro because he is one. No genuinely chivalrous white man would suffer a Negro to be openly robbed before his eyes on the street, nor would he without protest witness undue advantage taken openly of an ignorant Negro in the purchase of goods. Yet when the Negro raises a protest against mistreatment on the railway lines, it is often construed as an expression of undue assertion on his part, and as indicating a desire for riding in a mixed condition with the whites. So far as the present writer is informed, the separation is preferable to the Negro, provided the conditions be on an equitable basis of fare and comfort. The protest on the part of the Negro against unfair treatment no more means a craving for social equality than does his demand for value received in a mercantile establishment.

This bugbear of a desire on the part of the Negro for social equality, like certain others, exists chiefly in the imagination. When the Negro shall begin to publish books and papers in the interest of social equality, when he shall teach it in his schools, and inculcate it from his pulpits, then may we take cognizance of it, but not take counsel of our fears merely, and bring a railing accusation against the black man.

CHAPTER XVI.

OMENS OF PROMISE.

The years of race agitation in the South have not been without the production of certain results which are advantageous in their bearing on the future settlement of the question. Certain features have become distinct, every one of which is suggestive of the general course to be pursued in the final settlement of the problem. In addition to these are other existing indications which seem fraught with encouragement, among which may be named that of the growth of the division of sentiment among the whites of the states of the South. That is to say, while for a period there was no such division as was perceptible, there are those who are now the pronounced friends of the Negro, and the number is steadily increasing. Heretofore most of the discussions of the question were not altogether friendly to him, and many of them were decidedly unfavorable, many are rising up to be heard in his defense, from different points of observation. This is due to more than one cause, one of which is a growing conviction that the policy of repression so long pursued is in certain respects a mistaken one, and must be exchanged for one of encouragement and of incitement to attain to the utmost possibility of achievement.

That there is ability in the Negro race has been abundantly demonstrated. How much more clearly that demonstration might have been, but for the conditions of circumscription often imposed on the Negro cannot now be determined; but one thing is clearly manifest, namely, that the leadership developed by the race has been of manifold benefit in the direction of the forces of the race. More than it is aware, the public is indebted to that leadership for the frequent services rendered in directing the race away from courses from which society would have suffered had certain contingencies arisen. Fortunately, alike for the Negro and society at large, there is an unusual sanity which has all along dominated that leadership. While its course has excited the confidence of the race which it represents, it has commanded the esteem of all the white friends of the Negro. While those leaders might have seized on certain excited junctures for expressions of violence in order to stir improper passion, their policy has been to turn the gaze of the race to the possibilities of the future, and have sought to arouse its impulses to the performance of deeds which every sincere citizen has been forced to applaud. However much such leadership may have deplored certain violent and uncalled-for exhibitions, its influence has been thrown to the better side of turning each occasion to practical benefit. The influence of those leaders has been lent to peace and submission rather than to retaliation. The utter inutility of retaliation and its folly have been duly appreciated. To have been betrayed into a course of attempted retaliation would have occasioned an outbreak of interracial flames, the final result of which has been clearly foreseen by those in the front file.

True, these leaders have not escaped much harsh criticism at the hands of some, even of their own race, because of the pursuit of this policy, but it has been those of the more impetuous, who have failed to catch the ear of their people and have equally failed to win them from the direction of the more prudent and sagacious. While the notives of the wiser have not escaped impugnment, and while attempts have been made to reduce the strength of their influence with the masses of the race, their policy has been unchecked, their course unbroken. All this has not failed to attract the attention and to command the admiration of the more thoughtful of the whites, and has served to increase their zeal in behalf of the Negro race. The precipitation of tumult, no matter for what cause, would place the Negro at a tremendous disadvantage. Challenging the admiration and confidence of the better whites, who have shared in the disapprobation of the violence against the Negro, these same leaders have succeeded in building up increased interest in behalf of their race, the result of which has been that wrongs which were unnoticed at one time now claim profound attention and arouse deep indignation. By reason of conditions like these the loftier tone of sentiment in the South is steadily turning toward the welfare of the Negro race. From sources heretofore silent are now coming pronounced sentiments in favor of the Negro, and with a vigor and force which are destined to tell for good on the future of the colored race. In addition to this, the leading press of the country is manifesting signs of interest in the Negro's behalf which seem to promise much for his future good.

To two principal causes are the conditions now operating in the South, for interracial improvement, due. One of these is the emphatic worth of the Negro himself. He is becoming growingly useful in the varied pursuits into which he has entered, and in the accumulation of property, is becoming a taxpayer, and is showing increased interest in general affairs. His quiet and unostentatious attention to business, and his readiness to respond to any public or general good, are acting powerfully for the benefit of the race. This tendency is being met by a revival of interest in behalf of the Negro, which interest is being shown by the higher type of whites.

Another of the principal causes mentioned is due to a sociological change which was occasioned in the South in consequence of the chaotic conditions produced by the Civil War. With the overthrow of slavery in the South came the crash of its industrial system. Along with this, too, came a decline of the influence of the aristocratic class—the original slave owners. Then, too, with the subsidence, for a period of years, of this aristocratic influence, there came into partial and temporary prominence, men of a lesser class of influence whose conditions fitted them the more to grapple with the conditions of the tumultuous times than the men of the aristocracy. Many of this latter class, though far less powerful, came to political ascendancy and to the domination of public affairs. To this fact can be traced the decline of the power of the South in the leading councils of the nation. Once dominant in these high circles, the South has, for a period of years, been at a vast disadvantage because of the scarcity of its greater spirits among the leaders of the Union. Not in every instance, but in most, the politician of the South has succeeded the statesman of former days.

Now, there is a gradual reascendency of the better South. That higher and dominant class of other years is coming again to the front. There is a gradual revival of a long-suspended interest, and the immediate descendants of the element which once controlled the South are again rallying and resuming the station of influence.

This class has never ceased to be the friends of the Negro. He has never had sincerer friends than they. They have understood him as have no others. They know alike his weaknesses and his merits. Nor have they participated in the cruelties which have been visited on him. Most fortunate for the Negro is this reaction taking place just at this time, when the prospects of his people are brightening because of the conditions named several times in the discussion which has preceded. Nor are conditions wanting for bringing these forces into contact. While the leaders recognize the importance of keeping the race well within itself in its inherent progress, and while they recognize the necessity and the wisdom of the race thinking for itself rather than have another race to think for it, at the same time, it equally recognizes the importance of keeping in vital touch with the influential members of the stronger race. By means of this, there is an exchange of ideas from which comes a propulsion of force helpful to the Negro, and it may be said equally helpful to the philanthropic spirit of the white man.

The organization and steady growth of such helpful institutions of the Negro as the National Negro Business League, which was founded by President Booker T. Washington in 1900, have been of immense aid to the colored race of the country. This League was a healthful augury of Negro progress as the race entered the gateway of the new century. It is possibly the greatest concrete advertisement of Negro progress that has ever been conceived. The detailed presentation of the success of the men of the race who have accomplished much in the varied vocations awakens increased interest and effort, and speaks through the League, as a common medium, of the growth of its achievements.

Nor must we overlook such occasional assemblies as the Clifton Conference held at the summer home of Mr. W. N. Hartshorn, near Marblehead, Massachusetts, where were invited to meet together prominent men of both races, white and black, to discuss vital topics relative to the race question. The Conference had an additional significance when a prominent commander each of the opposing armies of the Civil War was present—Generals O. O. Howard, of Vermont, and R. D. Johnston, of Alabama, whose commands were directly opposite at Gettysburg. One of these was an original abolitionist and the other a large slave owner, yet they were here seated side by side in a conference of days to assist the black man in his dilemma. With these distinguished men sat the most prominent of the colored race in the same room, for days together, in the home of a quiet philanthropist, seeking means for the amelioration of the conditions of the colored people of the South.

These may be said to be among the silent forces, and so they are; and the outcome of the genius of these and other efforts will undoubtedly be slow, but they are at least the prophetic blooms of future fruit. Their silence and slowness give promise of ripeness and permanence. Agencies like these acting in cooperation with others less demonstrative, perhaps, but none the less efficacious, are serving to clear the way to a gradual solution of a question which has too long vexed the mind of the public. Emphasis given to movements like these continue to enhance in the public mind the importance of this vital subject. Nor does the steady growth of the progress of the Negro fail to win public attention. This does more than quicken public sympathy, it arouses substantial interest in the race. Every colored man who establishes himself in a useful and lucrative pursuit, widens the interest in behalf of his people.

Nor is the public unobservant of the efforts, most pathetic in themselves, on the part of the higher type of the Negro race, to reach and influence the baser elements of their people. Prompted by no other desire than that of the most generous philanthropy, thousands of the best are ministering in divers ways, daily, to the unfortunate of the race in a most quiet and unostentatious manner possible. They are not aware that this silent work is known and observed by those who are closely studying their conditions; yet it is known that in many sections there is a house to house ministration on the part of the best for the worst. It is doubtful if any other people on the globe are doing more with proportionate means at command than the Negroes of the South in genuine philanthropic effort. By means of hard earnings, eked out by the daily toil of thousands, the worthier are seeking to relieve and raise their unfortunate ones on the bottom rounds.

Until the condition of the Negro is studied in

detail, one fails to gain a genuine insight into what the majority of the Negroes are doing. In their own crude ways they are seeking to work from within outward for the improvement of their people, and such race loyalty has never been known as they exhibit. A people displaying a spirit like this is altogether worthy of encouragement, and it is gradually on the way.

So, notwithstanding the indulgence of certain morbid and lugubrious predictions concerning the race, its darkest days seem to be behind it. Difficulties great and grave are yet to be met, but the agencies now on the march, many of which are silent and without observation, give promise of their gradual removal. The Negro has a place in American life and cultivation, and he will eventually settle into it with a pluck to work out his destiny alongside that of the white race. It will not be by a fusion of the races, for against this the Negro is as firmly set as is his brother in white; but side by side the races will eventually live and thrive in mutual benefit and for the general good. Tendencies are concentrating toward this end, and calm wisdom will eventually find the proper path which will relieve the present stress by the discovery of a racial orbit for each, and racial adjustment will be fully consummated.

There will continue to be more or less violence on the lower basis of society, but the public is waking up to the fact that the preservation of society demands that this shall find an end, and so it will. So long as the race of Negroes proves its worth, as it is constantly doing, just so long will it continue to elicit the esteem of the better whites among them, and elsewhere. The Negro must work out his own destiny, as he has bravely set forth to do, and he will continue to command the encouragement of others about him. He has thousands of friends of whom he knows nothing, the interest of whom is stimulated by his commendable progress, and this will grow as he continues to show himself worthy. There are at present difficulties which seem impenetrable and which mock even the mildest form of optimism, but the hope of the situation lies in the application of the principles of the gospel concerning which Motley says: "Religion on all great historical occasions has acted as the most powerful of dissolvents." When the situation is cleared of its obscurity, which process is now in progress, Christian America will see in this question one that is without an equal in its appeal to heart and conscience from any point of view that it may be regarded.

Ten million human beings, whose presence in America is not one of choice, but one of coercion, with a history that is unique, and with a destiny which mightily relates itself to the permanent life of the nation, cannot be lightly esteemed. It shapes itself into a tremendous issue which carries with it a challenge alike to philanthropy and Christianity.

CHAPTER XVII.

A NEW DEMAND FOR AN "AGE OF REASON."

"Come, now, and let us reason together," was a divine injunction put into the lips of an ancient prophet to be voiced to a people who, swayed and controlled by the agitation of the times, had drifted far from duty and obligation. The preceding chapters have been prepared with a view of concentrating public attention on a stupendous question which towers in our midst, and in which inheres problems which must sooner or later be grappled with. Every one capable of even ordinary reflection is forced to a recognition of this as a mighty fact. Men of both races, white and black, see in the drift of present events and in the meanings which they bear on their surface, an inevitable increase of difficulty unless some policy can be devised for its solution. While this is true, there are certain plain principles which must inevitably push their way through the years of the future, and bear along with them certain results for good or evil, according to the direction which may now be given them. By no possible means can these principles be stemmed. The purpose should now be so to control and direct them that they may result in good and not in evil. The pliability of our institutions and the nature of our laws forbid the interposition of any policy other than that based on truth and justice in seeking to solve the present difficulty. The sooner this fact is recognized and acted on the better it will be for all concerned. There are hidden germs in the difficulty which have not yet come to life, and which when they shall do so, will mean immensely more than is now apparent in the augmentation of the race problem.

Drastic laws may prove a temporary makeshift in the present state of partially raw conditions, and the vent may be stopped thereby for a time, but meanwhile fresh complications are germinating, with a promise of future harvests. The attempted settlement of the difficulty has been deferred sufficiently long, and the problem has reached such proportions as to demand, it would seem, some prompt action. Let us calmly and quietly look at the situation and consider it in its varied relations to the future, for in its consideration we must be as profoundly concerned with respect to the future of this grave question as we are with it as it pertains to the present. It is a matter of concern, not to one more than to all. It is the one supreme American problem the baleful shadow of which is thrown toward the future of our prospective civilization.

It is well known that there is a prevailing idea that the Negro should be curtailed in his development and held within certain bounds. In some re-

gions this is a popular theory concerning our dealing with the Negro. We may advise, direct, and
assist, but cannot restrict. This is in opposition to
the laws of nature, and is destined to failure no
matter by whom attempted. In the very nature of
the case, we cannot set arbitrary boundaries to the
development of any race and say to such under inexorable edict—"Thus far shalt thou go, and no
further." An effort like this will carry with it its
own defeat and failure. The effort will beget fresh
forces and energies to its own undoing. Nothing is
plainer than this principle in all the past of human
history, and it is certainly patent in its application
to the present juncture. With the gateways of
opportunity and effort lying equally open to all alike,
the conclusion is apparent that a race of people who
have been able to achieve so much under the heavy
pressure of difficulty, the constant frown of opposition, and who have borne so successfully against the
inertia of complicated disadvantage, will accomplish
yet more as the momentum of success increases. In
the face of this fact it should be borne in mind that
this is but the beginning of the career of a new race
the accomplishments of which far exceed those of
any other of the colored races in America. This
progress cannot be checked, and will not. A success which enriches and improves the country, a
success which every one desires and applauds, will
not yield to any interdiction of opposition. While
this is true, under present conditions, with hostility

prevailing, this success is not without certain racial difficulties. This, it would seem, is a matter of necessary recognition even to the most casual observer.

A summary and violent disposal of the race question can never be. It is idle to cherish a dream like this. Its urgency may serve the present purpose of the mountebank, but to the solid citizen it is the veriest fatuity. The question, like all others, must be met on its merits. No harsh policy will avail. That would be nothing short of persecution which never fails of reaction. Persecution invariably returns with resounding and rebounding force. Certainly the Negro situation in the South is not one which calls for the exercise of any policy which approaches persecution. What would be its ground of excuse? What has the Negro done to invite it? Must he be persecuted for the services of centuries rendered as an enslaved man? Must he now be persecuted as a reward for his endurance and toil, and for his remunerative labor for generations? Is he now to become a victim of persecution because he served so well and so long in the development of the soils and mines of the country? Should the iron hand of persecution now grip him because he is striving to turn to practical account the grim disadvantages which meet him at every angle of his struggling march? Who that is prepared to say that he must not develop the powers of his efficiency to the highest degree possible, especially since by such efficiency he is made a more potent factor in the material enrichment of the country? By what possible law, human or divine, can this be done? To do this in republican America with any social group, any people among us, would require a recast of our institutions and a transformation of the genius of our government.

Set the boundaries as we may and hedge them about as we please with arbitrary circumscription, yet so long as our system of government is flexible, just so long will the superior and worthy Negro go beyond them and find a niche of his own making, where he will establish himself, and command respectful recognition. Nor is this meant to apply to social relations. The worthy and respectful Negro who dominates the rest in thought and sentiment, entertains no such vision. They claim that it would be unworthy of them and of the race to assert such claim. They are intent on erecting a worthy racial pride, and insist on the concentration of their people on this worthy purpose. They do ask for the exercise of simple justice in a free government, and for the consideration due them, and because of this they should excite our esteem. Social equality is a phantom born in the brain of the racial hater, and while it has been the occasion of much discussion, it has been found on investigation to be as baseless as a ghost story. Time and again, specters like that of social equality and of Negro ascendancy have come to disturb certain brains, but on examination they have been found to be without foundation.

Every thoughtful man must know that if even a fraction of the number of imaginary bugbears concerning the Negro had ever developed, the race would have long ago entered on the pathway of extinction. Nor is it this apprehension which deters the Negro from such assertion, it is because he has no such foolish dreams. He recognizes the fact that he must make for himself his own orbit of existence, he must build his own civilization under the auspices of an aspiring race, and to these ends his energies are directed without disturbing himself with concerns which are unpractical, unnatural, and unprofitable. Is it not true that as he proceeds the phantom of social equality recedes in the public mind? All along he has succeeded in setting over against adverse theories concerning himself, facts of worthiness.

Failing in all things else, resort is had to the theory of the rapid decline of the race as a possible fact by which the problem will be eventually solved and the land be rid of the Negro race. Certain works have been prepared in which this is held forth as a possible solution. If a theory like this be worthy of answer, a sufficient one is found in the fact that a race which has increased almost two million within a single decade shows but slight sign of diminution. It recalls the incident of the merchant who bought his matches at five cents a box and sold them at four, and when asked how he could do this, replied that it would be impossible did he not sell so many!

The fact that the Negro is submissive, and tractably accepts the situation—that he yields at one point, only to come again at another; that meanwhile he makes a place for himself in the heaving and tumultuous world and occupies it in thorough accord with well-defined laws of human progress; that his growth of efficiency multiplies the spheres of his adaptation of the world's demands, these are facts of enormous significance to which no thoughtful man can close his eyes. That the Negro by virtue of frugality and economy logically and naturally thrives, and that his services are so indispensably in demand, in itself, constitutes a fact that is prodigious if not portentous. For the moment forecasting the future, it requires no philosopher with microscopic sharpsightedness nor seer with acute discrimination to discover that to which the present will inevitably lead. If his advancement has been so rapid within the initial years of his freedom, in the future it will be more conspicuous. By reason of his well-known characteristics and his progress, it may be concluded that the darkest days of the Negro are now behind him. If he has succeeded under conditions so unfavorable. where he has not only encountered direct repression, but has shared in all the disasters, such as shortness of harvest and financial reverses, what may he not be expected to achieve within the next generation with an increased efficiency, widening observation, ripening experience, and deepening wisdom? Nor will this be done save in the ordinary way in which he has already succeeded as a planter, home builder, educator, author, artist, artisan, economist, banker, and professional man.

The achievements of the Negro have been quiet and undemonstrative. He has never been clamorous in the publication of his deeds to the world. Better would it be for him if these were more generally known. The worthy ones keep within themselves and are content to succeed without flaunting the facts in the face of the public. But the deeds of the unworthy are broadly known throughout the land, and the worthy ones must needs share in the opprobrium because all happen to belong to the same race. The progressive ones are content to labor on without inviting public recognition or without seeking applause. They have skill and learning, have sowed and reaped prosperously, have directed their affairs along legitimately commercial lines, have quietly built their homes, schools and churches, and established and maintained remunerative plants of divers kinds, all without demonstration and without interference with the affairs of the stronger race. Yea, thousands of them have found their way to a goodly degree of prominence without the elicit of local applause, without recognition, and sometimes encountering stout opposition. The aggregated results of Negro progress are enormous, as his taxable property of $600,000,000 attests. That the Negro by dint of exertion and well-recognized efficiency has so often made himself indispensable, in a variety of spheres for which he is so uniquely qualified, means much for the future of the race. In some of these spheres, because of his peculiar fitness and adaptability, he is preferred above all others. By common consent, any substitute, in certain spheres, would be unacceptable, so long as his services were available. The Negro is not blind to these facts and opportunities, and is not slow to appear on the scene at the proper time to use them to advantage. He may be decried and ridiculed, often is; his simple rights may be questioned, as is sometimes done; but the academic law of economics—demand and supply—comes to his rescue, and the question is oftenest settled, not by the Negro himself, but by those of the dominant race who need his services and pay for them.

Notwithstanding racial differences and friction, it is not uncommon to see Negroes and white men engaged in conversation about divers affairs in which they are mutually interested. Who sees members of the white race chatting with Chinamen, Japanese, Greeks or Italians? There is nothing in common between such, and there is nothing to talk about. These are facts of common observation and are not without credit to the Negro race among the colored races of America.

Consider another fact which relates to the future : the indulgence of racial prejudice serves to hold the races, as such, apart, the logical outcome of which is to discount the Negro purely on the basis of racial aversion. This naturally leads to imposition on the Negro race and to the taking of advantage of him by sheer force. Must it be suffered to escape us as a prospective fact, and one that is inevitable, that in the years of the future, when the Negro has become more learned and generally more efficient, with his power increased, we may deplore that we have allowed the opportunity to escape for making him our friend, and have made him our enemy instead? Because of the pressure of existing conditions, because of the exactions now imposed, he is steadily engaged in equipping himself, and is overcoming the barriers raised, in order to meet the requirement of the demands imposed.

Without entering the sphere of politics, save for the purpose of illustration, for politics has been studiously shunned throughout this discussion for obvious reasons, let attention be called, for the time, to a matter of practical interest alike to all. The bulk of the Negroes is now practically disfranchised in a number of the states, yet there are limits to which when he shall attain, he will be a qualified elector. He has dropped from view and is quietly accepting the situation and is fitting himself for future citizenship. When he shall reach the gateway of constitutional requirement, what will be his attitude to the

white race, if present conditions of race alienation
be suffered to go on? Shall he reach this stage the
friend or the enemy of the whites? Shall he be
permitted to bring with him to this goal a race hatred or a sentiment of friendliness? The present
purpose is not to discuss the restrictions imposed on
the ballot, but that of the relation of the races in
the future. Conditions now favor racial conciliation, and shall the policy be to continue a course
by which the Negro is estranged or shall it be to
make him the friend of the dominant race now, that
he may be such when he comes to citizenship? Now,
in certain quarters, it is unpopular even to espouse
the cause of the Negro in a temperate way, but is this
the policy of wisdom? It is not now claimed that
the result will be as indicated above, but it is worthy
of consideration just at this time, and in view of the
present drift. If the Negro be made our friend
now, he will be our friend then. He is now access-
ible, pliant, responsive. What assurance have we
that this will continue? It is evident that a policy
such as here advocated will be for the good of both
races alike. Shall the opportunity be now slighted?

It may be arrogantly said, in reply to this, that
this is a white man's country, and that he has nothing to fear. This is cheap talk and cheaper logic.
Granting all that may be implied in this boast, who
wishes to have in our midst a racial hostile minority,
when it can be avoided? Who is indifferent to the

multiplied and manifold complications permitted by ourselves to be transmitted to our children? Conceding that the Negro voter of the future may be beaten back, who is going to do the beating? If he be deceived, who is to practice the deception? If he is to be held down, who is going to remain down to do the holding? Does not this suggest future friction, and friction continually? Because one may chance to be physically and financially stronger than his next door neighbor, is he justified in the exercise of a hectoring spirit which requires perpetual vigilance of a suspicious nature, as well as time, energy, and the waste of moral strength, in order to hold his neighbor in abeyance and in awe? Who that covets an existence like this? Domination and preeminence are of small worth if they are to be adulterated with gall and vinegar.

The Negro is not without friends among the better whites of the South, who, as certain emergencies have arisen, have been heard with effect. The sentiment in his favor is not of the maudlin type, but it is a principle as solid as granite. Nor is it called into exercise because he is a Negro, but because he is a man.

Deep in the noblest type of the Anglo-Saxon character is the principle of loyalty to human opportunity and brotherhood, and in the states of the South are many who are possessed of this spirit. It is not the particular race which evokes this spirit, but principle, and the common cause of humanity. To this element of our chivalrous civilization the present question addresses itself with respect to conditions which now are, as well as to others which are liable to arise.

As the present writer sees it, no people ever enjoyed an advantage greater than that which is now offered the white race in its relation to the weaker race in these American states. Leaving out of view the unquestioned moral obligations which arise from the past and which have already been emphasized, it would seem the dictate of reason and of wisdom that we should now seek to make the most of the Negro, both for his good as well as for our own. That there could now be easily summoned to an undertaking like this the combined leadership of the Negro race in a policy of conciliation and of mutual helpfulness, there is no doubt, and that a course such as is here advocated would be helpful to all alike is beyond question. Why, then, should there be delay in the adoption of a movement which will rob the future of racial ominousness, and clear the years to come of inevitable difficulties with which other generations must grapple? To listen to the hoot of the racial hater and the clatter of the political pettifogger, who sees no further than his own temporary self-advantage, seems folly, in view of that which is involved as well as that which portends. Could a course justified by conditions well known be adopted for the relaxation of present conditions, and could there be established between the white and black races that which is friendly and tranquil, there could be but one result. Side by side there would eventually grow up a dual civilization in the American states, and especially in those of the South—one purely white American and the other Afro-American. As races they would keep within themselves, founding and maintaining each its own interests and institutions, and yet in spirit they would be combined. Each would be genuinely American, each would possess its own instincts and racial characteristics. While the races would not fuse, their interests would be in common. That which would be good for the one, would be equally so for the other. They would be "distinct as the billows, one as the sea." At multiplied points they would come into contact, but the better of each would sedulously and jealously guard the boundary of racial integrity. In such contact, under the same laws and beneath the same flag, with interests identical, harmony would hold sway and the land would prosper.

The dominant race faces an opportunity today which may decline with the present stage of advantage. On this race is imposed the duty of taking the initial step toward the realization of a condition which seems altogether possible. Unless it be done by the stronger race it cannot be done at all. As in the future there shall come to pass this dual condition of society in the American states' shall the races be friendly each to the other and work in adjustment for the good of each, or shall they be hostile? On this question, as on a common pivot, turns the Negro problem of the present as well as of the future.

INDEX

Advertiser, Montgomery (Ala.) quoted, 47.

Africa, resorted to, 29; slave market of the world, 120; relatio of American Negro to future of, 120; possibility of Christian ization of, 179.

Amalgamation opposed by the Negro, 216.

America, effect of its discovery on slave trade, 29; Negro's resi dence in, 74.

Apprehension unfounded, 188; unrealized, 199; two sources of, 211

Andrews, President E. Benj., quoted, 177.

Anglo-Saxon, achievements of the, 13; obligation of the, 38 indebtedness of the, 62; chief characteristic of the, 79; resort to the Negro, 82; progress during the last century, 114; kindl disposition of, 124; opportunity of the, 179; danger of self discredit, 204; present opportunity of, 230.

Arabs, as slave purchasers, 29.

Arbitration of Ga. R. R., 193.

Aristocracy, reassertion of Southern, 211; cause of its temporar decline, 212.

Attucks, Crispus killed at Boston, 74.

Augusta (Ga.) Chronicle quoted, 191.

Banks, Negro, 59.

Barton, Col., and his Negro aid, 75.

Barriers to Negro progress, 20; serious, 75.

Barrow, Chancellor D. C., alluded to, 190.

Birch, Samuel, alluded to, 91.

"Black Belt," the, 51.

Boston Transcript quoted, 192.

Boyd, Dr. R. F., alluded to, 98.

Boyd, Dr. R. H., alluded to, 98.

Browning, Mrs. quoted, III.

Bryce, Hon. James, quoted, 15.

Burden, where it lies, II.

Burke; Edmund, quoted, 52.

Census of 1900, showing of, 186.

Character, growth of appreciation of, 135; affected by conduct, 203.

Civilization involved, 168.

Civil War, 17, 23; the Negro during the, 63; his contribution to the, 64.

Chattanooga (Tenn.) Times quoted, 191.

Christianity, its duty to the Negro, 84; appealed to, 87; challenged by a condition, 142; hesitation, 151; plain duty of, 174; elevating power, 176; opportunity, 180; efficacy, 217.

Clifton Conference, 214.

Columbia (S. C.) State quoted, 191.

Confederacy, Southern Negro during the regime of, 63; Negro's relation to, 122.

Confidence, the Negro's hope, 97.

Constitution (Atlanta) quoted, 161.

Courier-Journal, (Louisville)) quoted, 161.

Crime denounced, II; source of, pointed out, 60.

Crisis in Negro's history, 21.

Darwin, alluded to, 115.

Demagogism and the Negro, 205.

Dober, the Moravian missionary to the West Indies, 145.

Dutch in South Africa, 14.

Education compared with other questions, 145; objection to Negro, 145; Negro strides in, 187; helpfulness of, to the Negro, 202.

Emancipation, mistaken view of, 17.

Encouragements to assist the Negro, 181; derived from his progress, 184.

England, change of policy of, 14; indebtedness to the American Negro, 83.

Enmity, source of, against the Negro, 22.

Equality, social, a bugbear, 104; groundlessness of its apprehension, 205; wholly subjective, 207; a specter, 222; its recession, 223.

Ethiopia alluded to, 149; number of its people, 189.

European immigration, menace of, 109.

Faneuil Hall, 74.

Fleming, Hon. W. H., quoted, 31.

Ft. Sumter alluded to, 81.

Galloway, Bishop Chas. B., quoted, 188.

INDEX

Geike, Cunningham, D. D., quoted, 91.

Georgia railroad strike, 189.

Gladstone alluded to, 115.

Gospel, its efficacy in seasons of juncture, 85.

Grant, President U. S., alluded to, 177.

Great Britain abolishes slavery, 79.

Groves, Junius G., "the potato king of Kansas," 98.

Hampton Institute alluded to, 201.

Hardwick, Hon. T. W., alluded to, 190.

Hartshorn, W. N., alluded to, 214.

Hebrew race, comparison with, 26; greatness of, 120.

Herbert, Hon. H. A., alluded to, 190.

Holmes, Oliver Wendell, alluded to, 115.

Home, the Negro's creation of the idea of, 137; its improvement and future promise, 138.

Hopkins, President Mark, quoted, 67.

Howard, Gen. O. O., alluded to, 214.

Illiteracy, reduction of, 144; its perils, 145.

Indiscrimination, unfairness of, 20; obscures merit, 42; unfortunate, 52.

Industry, indispensableness of, 134.

"Jim Crow" compartments, 206.

Johnston, Gen. R. D., alluded to, 214.

Justice, slumber of, 46; demanded for, 48; denied, 72; character of, illustrated, 148.

Land owners, Negro, 184.

Leaders Negro, and the saloon, 19; distinguished, 49; early development of, 52; wisdom of, 54; merit of, 55; onerous task of, 93.

Lee, Gen., relation to the feat of a Negro, 75.

Legislation, drastic, its effects, 203; what it forecasts, 219.

Lincoln, Abraham, alluded to, 115.

Lovett, Judge Robt. S., quoted, 196.

Lowell quoted, 48.

Lynching practically unknown in former years, 153; its immediate consequences, 154; its failure to accomplish the end proposed, 155; its claims absurd, 156; its assumption, 157; defiance of the judiciary, 159; reckless lawlessness, 160; illustrated, 162; injustice shown, 163.

Magnanimity needed, II.

Marblehead Mass., 214.
Massachusetts abolishes slavery, 79.
Massey, Gerald, quoted, 94.
Mendelssohn, Felix, alluded to, 115.
Middle States, indebtedness of, to Negro, 66; enjoying the fruits of his toil, 83.
Moffatt, the missionary, alluded to, 169.
Moravian missions, 145.
Moses alluded to, 90.
Motley, John Lothrop, quoted, 217.
Murphy, E. G., quoted, 48; alluded to, 157, 158.
National Negro Business League, a happy conception, 129; founded, 213.
Negro, relation to American life, 12; effect of aiding him, 12; proposals concerning him, 23, 24; his contribution to the solution of the problem, 24; advancement of, 25; standard of comparison, 27; not a voluntary immigrant, 29; imposition on, 32; how he came to be in America, 36; unfairness to, 37; his position, 40; his disposition, 40; mistreatment of, 41; North and South compared, 43; different classes of, 51; unjust discrimination against, 52; varied classes, 53; leaders among, 55; struggles after education, 57, 58; criminal class, 59; seen at his worst, 61; loyalty and devotion, 63, 64; indebtedness to, 65; treatment during slavery, 66; achievments, 69; worthy of aid, 70; in the Revolution, 76; services during the Civil War, 77; wrangles over the, 78; characteristics compared, 79; why brought South, 80; labor demanded, 82; struggles, 85; contribution to civilization, 86; disadvantages of, 88; drawbacks, 89; difficulties aggravated, 90; stigma on the, 91; contact with Anglo-Saxon, 91; material progress of, 92; his pluck, 92; leaders as pioneers, 93; racial pride needed, 95; mistaken notion concerning his leadership, 96; his reliance, 96; is he worth while?, 100; considerations in favor of, 101; opposition to, 102; only source of labor, 103; value to our civilization, 105; producer of wealth, 106; protection to Southern society, 108; advancement of, 110; predictions concerning the, 111; compared with the white race, 112; hidden possibilities, 115; religious devotion, 116; considerations favorable to helping the, 117; obligations to, 118; his tractableness, 119; a new race, 120; cheerfulness, 121; characteristics, 123; courage, 125; adjustability,

126; not turbulent, 127; awakens esteem by his worth, 129; obstructions, 130; womanhood, 131; race patriotism, 136; worth exhibited, 139; vindication of worth, 140; ridicule of, 147; cruelty to, 148; advantage afforded by his progress, 173; his responsiveness, 174; worthy of encouragement, 177; discrimination against, 178; progress of, illustrated, 193; lessons from experience, 199; challenges by worth, aid and support, 215; his philanthropy, 215; his place in American life, 216; must work out his own destiny, 217; intent on preserving racial pride, 222; future work, 223; general disposition, 224.

Negro question, discussion of, 9; a problem, 28; dangers of, 45.

Negro race, integrity of, 133; its decline a mistake, 223; rapid advancement, 224; quiet and undemonstrative, 225; its financial assets, 226.

New England and slavery, 30; alluded to, 66; relation of to Southern cotton, 80; indebtedness to the Negro, 83.

New Jersey abolishes slavery, 79.

New York abolishes slavery, 79; Evening Post quoted, 192; World quoted, 192; Tribune quoted, 193.

Nile's Register quoted, 77.

Nitzschamann, the Moravian missionary, alluded to, 146.

North, Negro in the, 44.

Paul alluded to, 150.

Persecution, 221.

Pharisaism condemned, 150.

Policy, sane, needed, 218; mistaken, 219.

Pennsylvania abolishes slavery, 80.

Pettiford, Dr. W. R., beginning in the banking business, 98.

Philippines alluded to, 14.

Poe, Edgar Allan, alluded to, 115.

Politics, a phase of, 227.

Predictions disappointed, 197.

Poor, Salem, honorable mention made of, 75.

Prejudice, 50; or piety, 73; proposal of, 117; illustrated, 150; force of, 150; possible consequences of, 183; removed by worthiness, 201; a detriment, 227.

Prince, a Negro, captures Gen. Prescott, 75.

Problem, source of, 28; development of, 34; a forecast of greater, 45; is not the Negro's, 142; national, 143; gravest before the American people, 219.

Progress, Negro, illustrated, 185; has been quiet, 186; cannot be checked, 220.

Providence, operation of, 39; and history, 46; relation to the Negro, 86; commits the Negro to the care of the white race, 149.

Question, race, not exclusively for the South, 143; cannot be settled by violence, 221.

*Races, and issues inseparable, 203; the two, will thrive side by side, 216; mutual relationship between the, 226; relations possible in the future, 228; possible pitfalls between the, 229; friendliness between, indispensable, 232.

Racial antipathy, 151.

Reconstruction era, horrors of, 18; imposition on the Negro, 89; its condemnation, 177.

Repression, effect of, 11; and construction, 24.

Revels, Senator, letter of, 177.

Rivalry, fears of industrial, baseless, 204.

Roosevelt, President, alluded to, 161.

Salem, Peter, kills Major Pitcairn, 75.

Saloon, effects of on the Negro, 18.

San Juan Hill, battle of, 125.

Sentiment, public, against the Negro, 152; changed by conditions, 197; efforts to warp, 198.

Shaler, Prof. N. S., quoted, 43.

Silent forces, operation of, 214.

Slavery discussed, 31; effects of, 32; former defense of, 33; its snares, 34; iniquity of, 46; arguments in favor of, 67; indebtedness to Christianity, 84; stigma of, 91; effects of, on the race, 133.

Society for Promoting Christian Knowledge, 178; for Propagating the Gospel in Foreign Parts, 178.

South, the, her desolation, 143; a double obligation imposed, 144; what she has done for Negro education, 144; cause of decline in national councils, 212; society of the, recognizing necessity of action, 216.

South Africa, 14.

Stephens, Hon. Alex. H., "corner stone speech," 81.

Taylor, Rev. Preston, the preacher financier, 98.

Tennyson, alluded to, 115.

Todd, Harry, his wealth, 98.

Tuskegee Institute alluded to, 201.

Vermont abolishes slavery, 79.

irtue commended, 133.

Washington, Dr. Booker T., quoted, 44; beginning at Tuskegee, 97; position stated, 135; quoted, 203; founder of National Negro Business League, 213.

West Indies, missions in the, 145.

White race, duty of in the present crisis, 166; its coöperation needed, 167; beneficiary of Negro labor, 172.

Womanhood, genuine, hope of the Negro race, 131; imposition on Negro, 132; safeguards needed, 133; influences against, 139; genuine, needed in present juncture, 141.

Year 1809, notableness of, 114.

www.ingramcontent.com/pod-product-compliance
Lightning Source LLC
Chambersburg PA
CBHW040826300326
41914CB00058B/1185